Negotiating and Implementing a North American Free Trade Agreement

Negotiating and Implementing a North American Free Trade Agreement

Edited by Leonard Waverman

The Fraser Institute/Centre for International Studies
Vancouver, British Columbia/Toronto, Ontario, Canada

Canadian Cataloguing in Publication Data

Main entry under title:

Negotiating and implementing a North American free trade agreement

Includes bibliographical references.
ISBN 0-88975-139-0

1. Free trade—Canada. 2. Free trade—United States. 3. Free trade—Mexico. 4. North America—Economic integration. I. Waverman, Leonard, 1941– II. Fraser Institute (Vancouver, B.C.)
HF1766.N43 1992   382'.917   C92-091040–8

Printed in Canada.

Contents

Introduction

The central preoccupation of the Fraser Institute and its research program is the solutions that markets provide for the economic problems that are mankind's constant companion. Government-imposed impediments to free markets frequently injure those they are intended to help and benefit groups who in turn become the champions of the political support for the impediments. Protectionism is undoubtedly one of the more insidious of these anti-market devices. The beneficiaries of protection are often concentrated politically, and are therefore effective in pressing their case. The victims of protectionism—consumers of the protected product—are diffuse in their interest, and disorganized in pressing their own case. Consequently, protectionism has been a constant source of economic loss.

This book contains a set of studies dealing with institutions and procedures that affect North American economic integration including legal institutions which either facilitate or hamper freer trade in North America. Several of the papers provide a historical outline of North American trade negotiations that have taken place to date and assess issues involved in moving towards a trilateral free trade agreement. It is an output of an extensive program of research and other activities which the Fraser Institute has undertaken in conjunction with the Centre for International Studies at the University of Toronto, the Hudson Institute, the Center for Strategic and International Studies, Political Economy Research Center, El Colegio de Mexico, and economists at many of the most prestigious universities on the continent. This four-year program of activity has been generously funded by the Lilly Endowment, Inc. of Indianapolis and we are pleased to acknowledge their wholehearted support and the encouragement and insights that have been provided by John Mutz and Gordon St. Angelo.

There can be no more important set of issues than those that relate to the establishment of one market for most products on the North American continent. The Fraser Institute has therefore been pleased to lend its support and assistance to the accomplishment of this program of research which reaches out for an understanding of how North America will be configured as we begin to recognize the opportunities of the next century. However, the authors in this book and in all of the other projects in the program of the Fraser Institute work independently and are subject to review only by independent referees and editors. In consequence, the conclusions to which they come are their own and may or may not reflect the view of the members or the Trustees of the Fraser Institute.

Steven Globerman

Preface

The Canada-USA Free Trade Agreement (CAFTA) liberalizes trade in goods and services and contains a number of novel instruments to handle trade disputes between the two countries. However, a number of very important trade issues were *not* dealt with to any great extent in the CAFTA. Some of these issues, such as the subsidies code, were left with a given deadline, in this case five to seven years, to come up with a new process. Other issues were not dealt with at all. Thus the Canada-USA Free Trade Agreement, although a crucial step in the direction of freeing trade in goods and services and in capital and labour markets in North America, was not the final end in the process. Now that serious negotiations are taking place between Canada, USA and Mexico on a North America Free Trade Agreement (NAFTA), questions arise as to how CAFTA could be expanded to incorporate Mexico and whether, alternatively, a parallel agreement would have to be signed.

In this volume six papers address some of these issues. Leading scholars produce very insightful analyses of where we are in trade liberalization and the obstacles still remaining to freer trade and investment. While the topics are somewhat disparate, together they provide a most useful and thoughtful analysis of crucial issues of trade relations in North America.

Gary Horlick and Amanda DeBusk examine the functioning of the dispute resolution panels which were established under Chapters 18 (safeguard) and 19 (countervail and antidump) of the Canada-USA Free Trade Agreement. One of the major Canadian desires in the FTA was secure access to the U.S. market. Canadian officials felt that Canadian industry had been harassed by the use of antidump and countervail measures in the USA in the early part of the 1980s. However, rather than arriving at a subsidies code, a joint bilateral definition of subsidies and the abandoning of countervail and antidump measures aimed at each other, Canada and the USA came up with a novel solution--*binational dispute resolution*.[1]

Horlick and DeBusk examine how these Chapter 18 and 19 systems have functioned over the first two years of operation. The authors show that dispute resolution under the FTA is more than twice as fast as would be the

---

1   *These binational panels came under a lot of discussion before they actually met and examined cases. It was unclear to many observers whether these panels would provide a substantial change in the administration of U.S. trade "remedies" and thus their perceived benefits to Canada were questioned.*

case were these decisions appealed to the U.S. judicial system. More importantly, the panel decisions in several countervail cases have had material impacts on the process where complaints are heard and decisions made at the initial level by the International Trade Commission in the United States. The reason for this beneficial impact is simple: now every case decided by the ITC can be reviewed by a bilateral dispute panel. The new review process then constrains the ability to use certain arguments before the ITC. Therefore Horlick and DeBusk argue that in effect more secure access to U.S. markets was obtained by Canada.

The paper by Bello and Winham examines the process by which private sector interest groups were brought into the negotiations process in the United States and Canada. Bello and Winham also examine the role of the media and the impact of public opinion on the results of the 1988 Canadian election which was fought over the FTA.

Bello and Winham show that the USA had a well established process (too well established for a number of observers) which allowed private sector input into the negotiating process of the FTA. The authors analyze the structure by which private sector input can be formalized in the USA and examine the influence this input had on negotiations and perhaps on the results in various key sectors--automobiles, alcoholic beverages, fish, lobsters, potatoes and lumber. Canada had no formal process which involved private interest groups in trade talks until January 1986 when the Canadian government established ITAC, the International Trade Advisory Committee, basically modelled after the U.S. process. Bello and Winham suggest that the U.S. and Canadian processes both channel and contain private interest pressures. It is important to highlight the second part of this (containment), for many people consider private interest groups as naturally being opposed to free or liberalized trade. (This of course is not true.) A formal structure of *broad* advisory groups with real input to the process includes those who are opponents of free trade as well as those in favour. It is more difficult for private interest groups to affect decisions at this broad level than through private and secret lobbying.

Bello and Winham also discuss the importance of public opinion and how it greatly affected the negotiations. They question whether anything has been learnt from the distortions that appeared in Canada over the public debate over the FTA.

Jeff Schott and Gary Hufbauer examine how one could move from a Canada-USA FTA to a Canada-USA-Mexico agreement. They begin by discussing several issues which were not dealt with fully in the FTA and which could be dealt with in new negotiations with Mexico. (The Canadian position is that the FTA cannot be reopened on any account.) They discuss intellectual property, subsidies, countervail and antidump and analyze what, in their view, could be done to improve the FTA. In moving to a trilateral FTA they examine the issues they see as crucial to its development--rules of origin, energy, and cultural industries. They then turn to an important discussion of whether a truly trilateral agreement is feasible or whether there will be separate bilateral deals. They are of the opinion that the dispute settlement process discussed by Horlick and DeBusk could be expanded to include Mexico "if Mexico aligns its administrative procedures to U.S. and Canadian norms in terms of open proceedings and written opinions " (page 76). They end their paper with a discussion of an "accession" clause so that other countries in the western hemisphere could join the agreement without having to go through this process again.

The paper by Peter Morici examines transition mechanisms and safeguards in a trilateral North American Free Trade Agreement. Adding Mexico provides increased competition for a number of Canadian and U.S. producers and the ability to undertake, within a broader North America, the kind of outsourcing and technological shifts that have occurred in Asia. Professor Morici is less sanguine than most other economists about the potential for great income gains to Canada and the USA through adding Mexico, although he thinks that for Mexican income growth, a NAFTA is necessary. As he says "the outcome will depend heavily" on the skills of workers in Canada and the United States and how they compare to those in Japan, Western Europe and Mexico (page 92). These skills are dependent on their educational level and efficiency--certainly not achievements at present that lead to great optimism. Morici stresses that a well thought out and formal transition mechanism is absolutely necessary if NAFTA is to become a political reality and an economic success. The transition mechanism is discussed under a number of elements--tariffs, quantitative restrictions, special provisions for horticultural products and whether bilateral or global safeguards are superior. Morici provides specific recommendations in these areas including explicit phase-out periods.

Arndt, Kaempfer and Willett examine the thorny issues of subsidies and countervailing duties in the context of North America. They remind us that the issues of subsidies and their controls are a vexing issue not only within North America but at the global level and in GATT. They discuss why this issue was not dealt with in CAFTA (because of conflicting policy objectives and the uncertainty of how these issues would be handled at a regional level when they are perceived of as a world problem). They examine current U.S. procedures in countervailing duty cases and a set of alternatives that could be utilized. Many of these alternatives have appeared in the academic press. One idea presented by a number of people is to increase the deminimis rate of foreign subsidization needed to trigger U.S. policy from the current 0.5% to, say, 1.0%. Other ideas are to change the definition of the injury from a gross to a net definition and include the impacts on consumers, a group that does not appear at the moment in CVD determinations in the United States. The authors examine the use of subsidies in the place of duties and analyze the case for the country with the alleged injury rebating CVD duties. These, however, are not really realistic solutions. They end with a discussion of the difficulties that will be faced in handling subsidies in a trilateral context; this is a discussion that does not generate much optimism on the part of the reader.

The final chapter of this volume deals with nontariff barriers in North America. Murray Smith classifies these nontariff barriers into three general areas: border measures, trade laws and internal measures. Included in the first category are issues such as rules of origin; in the second are antidump and CVD and in the third are the issues of intellectual property, procurement, etc. This is a formidable array of domestic policies to consider examining within a trilateral framework. As in the previous papers on subsidies and countervail, Smith argues that it is necessary to have linkages to the multilateral process since many of these issues spill over the North American context and really have to be dealt with at a higher level.

Rules of origin are going to be the most vexing issue in border measures. Rules of origin were a difficult concept to negotiate in the FTA and will be made much more difficult by adding Mexico, especially since some of the parties to the FTA wish to change what they have already agreed to. The auto sector is the most contentious area of all and here there are clear differences between the three countries with U.S. producers wanting higher rules of origin than in the FTA, Canada wanting no change and Mexico likely wanting lower rules of origin. Who will win out is difficult to see. Smith also discusses dumping, subsidies and national treatment and suggests the need for new mechanisms in these areas and in dealing with NTBs. Instead of trilateralizing issues such as subsidies he argues that one can retain domestic subsidy policies but by raising the criteria to which they are applied to the partner countries, remove most of their noxious elements. This is an excellent idea. Another approach discussed involves some form of joint administration of unilateral import relief laws. This is not likely to be seen in our generation. Finally, Smith turns to examining environmental measures--these are now being labelled by some as "green protection"; Canadian lobsters have been kept out of U.S. markets on the grounds that they were being caught too small and therefore imports to the USA would deplete the Canadian stock. Mexican tuna has been kept out of the U.S. markets on the basis that the methods of catching them also catches dolphins. Mexico has complained to GATT and has recently won. As we solve old protectionist measures we can be confident that industries will find new means of protection.

These essays tell us that the road to extending CAFTA to incorporate true remedies to issues such as CVD and antidump is difficult. Equally treacherous is the path to add Mexico to CAFTA. However, we have accomplished much and the difficulties ahead show the gains that can be achieved. These gains are important to our future and require pathbreaking remedies to the trade barriers that still divide us.

Leonard Waverman

About the Authors

Gary N. Horlick

Gary Horlick is a partner in the Washington office of O'Melveny & Myers, specializing in international trade matters. Prior to that, he served as Deputy Assistant Secretary of Commerce (where he was responsible for the administration of the U.S. antidumping and countervailing duty laws, the foreign trade zones program, and other statutory import programs), as International Trade Counsel for the Senate Finance Committee, and practices international trade law in Washington. He taught international trade law at Yale Law School for three years, and now teaches that subject at Georgetown Law Center. He is a graduate of Dartmouth College, Cambridge University, and Yale Law School; he was born and lives in Washington, D.C.

F. Amanda DeBusk

Amanda DeBusk has practised international trade before the International Trade Commission, the International Trade Administration of the Department of Commerce and the Office of the United States Trade Representative, and international trade litigation before the Court of International Trade. She has worked in export licences before the International Trade Administration of the Department of Commerce, the Defense Department, the State Department and the Coordinating Committee for Multilateral Export Controls. She is presently an associate at O'Melveny & Myers. She is a member of the International Trade Section of the D.C. Bar and the International Law and Practice Section of the American Bar Association, and has a J.D. from Harvard University.

Judith Hippler Bello

Judith Hippler Bello is employed by Sidley & Austin in international trade practice. She has been a member of President Bush's Commission on Federal Ethics Law Reform; General Counsel, Chairman and Deputy General Counsel for the Office of the U.S. Trade Representative; Deputy for Policy for the Department of Commerce; Attorney Advisor and Deputy Agent of the United States for the Department of State. She has been visiting lecturer at Yale Law School and Adjunct Professor at Georgetown University Law Center. Among her professional activities, she has been a

Co-Chairman for the American Bar Association, a Chairman for the D.C. Bar, and on the Editorial Advisory Board of the American Society of International Law's *International Legal Materials*. Judith Bello has testified before various Congress committees, been a featured speaker in international broadcasts, and lectured widely throughout the United States. Her publications include *Guide to the U.S.-Canada Free Trade Agreement*, *The Antidumping and Countervailing Duty Laws: Key Legal and Policy Issues*, and numerous articles. She has a J.D. from Yale Law School.

Gilbert R. Winham

Gilbert R. Winham is Professor of Political Science at Dalhousie University and in 1990/1 served as the Claude T. Bissell Visiting Professor of Canadian-American Relations at the University of Toronto. He received a Diploma in International Law from the University of Manchester in 1965 and a Ph.D. from the University of North Carolina at Chapel Hill in 1968. He is a member of the International Trade Advisory Committee (ITAC) and chaired a Task Force of that body on GATT Institutional Reform. Professor Winham has served on two FTA Dispute Settlement panels and he was a Research Coordinator for International Political Economy for the Macdonald Royal Commission. He conducts training simulations of trade negotiations for developing country trade officers at the GATT on a semi-annual basis. Professor Winham has authored articles and books on international trade policy and negotiations, including *International trade and the Tokyo Round Negotiation*, 1986 and *Trading With Canada: The Canada-US Free Trade Agreement*, 1988.

Jeffrey J. Schott

Jeffrey J. Schott is a research fellow at the Institute for International Economics in Washington. He has also concurrently been an Adjunct Professor of International Business Diplomacy at Georgetown University in the School of Foreign Service. He was formerly a senior associate at the Carnegie Endowment for International Peace, an official of the US Treasury Department in the areas of international trade and energy policy and, during the Tokyo Round of multilateral trade negotiations, he was a member of the U.S. delegation that negotiated the GATT Subsidies Code. Jeffrey Schott is the author or coauthor of several recent books on trade, including *North American Free Trade: Issues and Recommendations* (forthcoming), *Completing the Uruguay Round*, *Free Trade Areas and U.S. Trade Policy*, *The Canada-United States Free Trade: The Global Impact*, *Auction Quotas and United States Trade Policy*, and *Trading for Growth: The Next Round of Trade Negotiations*, as well as numerous articles on U.S. trade policy and the GATT. Mr. Schott holds an MA degree with distinction in international relations from the School of Advanced International Studies, Johns Hopkins University.

Gary C. Hufbauer

Gary C. Hufbauer is the Marcus Wallenberg Professor of International Financial Diplomacy at Georgetown University and Visiting Fellow at the Institute for International Economics. A Harvard and Cambridge graduate, he has published 16 books and numerous scholarly articles on international trade, finance and tax policy. From 1977 to 1980 he served as Deputy Assistant Secretary in the U.S. Treasury where he was responsible for trade policy during the Tokyo Round. A member of the bar in the District of Columbia in Maryland, he has been Director of the International Tax Staff at the U.S. Treasury, Deputy Director of the International Law Institute, Visiting Professor of Economics at Cambridge and the Stockholm School of Economics, and advisor and consultant to various governments and corporations.

Peter Morici

Peter Morici is a Professor of Economics at the University of Maine, and an adjunct Senior Fellow at the National Planning Association and the Iacocca Institute. An acknowledged expert on U.S. international trade policy and North American economic integration, he is the author of seven books and many monographs and journal articles. His most recent books are *Trade Talks with Mexico: A Time for Realism* and *Making Free Trade Work: The Canada-U.S. Agreement*. Later this year, *A New Special Relationship: The Free Trade Agreement and U.S.-Canada Commercial Relations* will be published jointly by the Institute for Research on Public Policy in Halifax and the Carleton University Centre for Trade Policy and Law in Ottawa.

Sven W. Arndt

Sven W. Arndt is Professor of Economics and Director of the Lowe Institute of Political Economy at Claremont McKenna College. He is President of the Commons Institute for International Economic Studies and editor of *Commons Sense*. He has authored and edited a number of books, including *The Competitiveness of the U.K. Economy* and *Real-Financial*

Linkages Among Open Economies, and a number of journal articles including "Adjustment in the Process of Trade Liberalization: The U.S. and Mexico" and "EC 1992 from a North American Perspective."

William H. Kaempfer

William H. Kaempfer is an Associate Professor of Economics at the University of Colorado at Boulder. He holds a Ph.D. from Duke University and has also taught at the Claremont Graduate School, Claremont McKenna College and the University of Washington. In recent years he has published several theoretical and empirical studies in trade policy analysis including work in the *American Economic Review, Economic Letters, Kyklos* and *International Organization*. In particular, he has written extensively on international economic sanctions. This work will be the focus of a forthcoming book, *International Economic Sanctions: A Public Choice Study*, to be published by Westview Press in 1992.

Thomas D. Willett

Thomas D. Willett is a graduate of the College of William and Mary and the University of Virginia. He is currently Horton Professor of Economics at the Claremont Graduate School and Claremont McKenna College, and also serves as Director of the Claremont Institute for Economic Policy Studies and Associate Director of the Lowe Institute of Political Economy. He previously taught at Cornell and Harvard and served on the senior staff of the Council of Economic Advisors and as Director of International Research for the U.S. Treasury. He is coeditor of *Economic Inquiry* and has served on the editorial boards of nine other journals. He also edits a series on The Political Economy of the Global Interdependence for Westview Press. A specialist in the areas of international economics and the political economy of economy policy, he is author of over 100 books and articles. His recent books include *The Political Economy of International Organization* coedited with Roland Vaubel, *Monetary Policy for a Volatile Global Economy, International Trade Policies* coedited with John Odell, and *Political Business Cycles* and *Exchange Rates, Trade and the U.S. Economy* coedited with Sven Arndt and Richard J. Sweeney.

Murray G. Smith

Murray Smith became the Director of the Centre for Trade Policy and Law, Carleton University and the University of Ottawa, September 1, 1990.

Previously, he was Director of the International Economics Program of the Institute for Research on Public Policy from June 1987. Before that, he was with the C.D. Howe Institute, where he served as a Senior Policy Analyst and Canadian Research Director for the Canadian-American Committee. During the Tokyo Round of multilateral negotiations, he was Director of International Economic Relations in the British Columbia government. He is author or coauthor of several books and articles on international economic issues. He is coauthor of *Taking the Initiative: Canada's Trade Options, Bridge the Gap: Trade Laws in the Canada-U.S. Negotiations*, and *Global Imbalances and U.S. Policy Responses*. He is editor of *Canada, the Pacific & Global Trade*, examining proposals for cooperation among Pacific economies in the context of Europe's 1992 agenda and the Uruguay Round of multilateral negotiations. His most recent publications are as editor of *Global Rivalry and Intellectual Property: Developing Canadian Strategies*. He serves on the roster of panellists for disputes under Chapter 18 of the Canada-USA Free Trade Agreement.

Leonard Waverman

Leonard Waverman is a Professor in the Department of Economics, University of Toronto, and Director of the University's Centre for International Studies. He received his B.Comm. and M.A. from the University of Toronto (1964 and 1965 respectively) and his Ph.D. from MIT in 1969. He has been a visiting scholar at the University of Essex, Stanford University and the Sloan School at MIT. Dr. Waverman specializes in industrial organization, and anti-trust, energy and telecommunications economics. He has authored numerous scholarly works, was a Board Member of the Ontario Energy Board, and currently is a Board Member of the Ontario Telephone Service Commission. He has consulted widely in both Canada and the USA. He has been the editor of *The Energy Journal* since the beginning of 1990. He has also been an associate editor of the *Canadian Journal of Economics* and has served on the Executive Committee of the European Association for Research in Industrial Economics. In 1991 he was a Visiting Professor at INSEAD in Fountainebleau, France. Forthcoming publications include an examination of Costs and Productivity in the U.S., Canadian, Japanese and German Automobile Industries (joint with Mel Fuss: Cambridge University Press); analyses of USA/Canada/Mexico Free Trade (for the Economic Council of Canada); an analysis of costs and regulation in European satellite service provision (joint with Hendrik Roller: for Eutelsat); and an analysis of the system of international telecommunications pricing (for the OECD).

Chapter 1

The Functioning of FTA Dispute Resolution Panels

Gary N. Horlick and F. Amanda DeBusk[1]

Introduction

Dispute resolution panels are one of the main underpinnings of the Canada-USA Free Trade Agreement ("FTA").[2] During the negotiation of the FTA, Canada and the United States ("the Parties") sought to negotiate common rules for dealing with subsidies and dumping. However, they were unable to agree. There were political problems, and the time period to negotiate such rules was extremely short. Most importantly, the United States could not agree to discipline its domestic subsidies on a bilateral basis. The dispute resolution mechanism of Chapter 19 represents the resulting compromise. Under Chapter 19, trade disputes concerning antidumping and

---

1   The views in this article are those of the authors, reflecting in large part their experience with six of the FTA panels, and do not necessarily reflect the views of their clients. The authors would like to thank Edward K. Kwakwa, Esq., Robert S. Klein, Lucius B. Lau, Michael A. Meyer, and Rebecca Stack for their assistance in preparing this article.

2   Canada-United States Free Trade Agreement, Jan. 2, 1988, U.S.T. ____, T.I.A.S. No. ____, reprinted in 27 I.L.M. 281 (1988).

countervailing duty investigations may be resolved by a panel of experts from both nations as a substitute for judicial review.[3]

In addition to providing a dispute resolution mechanism for dumping and countervailing duty cases, the FTA provides in Chapter 18 a binding means for resolving disputes involving "safeguard" import relief. Chapter 18 also covers other types of disputes under the FTA and permits Canada and the United States to use Chapter 18 as a substitute for the General Agreement in Tariffs and Trade ("GATT")[4] dispute resolution. The Chapter 18 panels have broad jurisdiction[5] to consider disputes with two exceptions. Chapter 18 panels cannot be invoked for either financial services issues (which are governed by Chapter 17 of the FTA) or for final decisions in antidumping and countervailing duty cases (which are governed by Chapter 19 of the FTA).

This article explores how the Chapter 18 and Chapter 19 panel systems have functioned over their first two years of operation.[6] It concludes that the panels have been quite successful in achieving the FTA goals of timely and impartial decisions.[7]

3 *See* 19 U.S.C. § 1516a(g) (1988) concerning the review of countervailing duty and antidumping duty determinations involving Canadian merchandise; *see also* Special Import Measures Act, § 77.11(2), as amended S.C. 1988, c. 65, concerning the review of countervailing duty and antidumping duty determinations involving U.S. merchandise.

4 1 Supp. BISD 6 (1953).

5 Specifically, Chapter 18 panels have jurisdiction over "the avoidance or settlement of all disputes regarding the interpretation or application of [the FTA] or whenever a Party considers that an actual or proposed measure of the other Party is or would be inconsistent with the obligations of [the FTA] or cause nullification or impairment in the sense of Article 2011, unless the Parties agree to use another procedure in any particular case." FTA Article 1801(l). Article 2011 provides that if any measure causes nullification or impairment of any benefit reasonably expected to accrue to Canada or the United States, either country can invoke the Chapter 18 dispute resolution process even though the measure does not directly conflict with obligations under the FTA. FTA Article 2011(l).

6 There are other dispute resolution mechanisms in the FTA as well, such as those in Chapter 7 concerning agricultural disputes, but this article is limited to chapters 18 and 19.

7 Binational Panel Reviews and Extraordinary Challenge Committees; United States-Canada Free-Trade Agreement, 53 Fed. Reg. 53,212 (1988); *see also* House Comm. on the Judiciary, United States-Canada Free-Trade Agreement Implementation Act of 1988, H.R. Rep. No. 816, 100th Cong., 2d Sess., pt. 4, at 3 (1988) (the arbitral system's advantages of quickness and low cost will help the parties calculate the economic costs and benefits involved in appealing a case); Testimony of Charles F. Doran, Director, Center of

Overall, the panel decisions have been well-written and thoughtful. The process for establishing the panels has functioned smoothly and both countries have given binding effect to the decisions. There has been one challenge of a Chapter 19 panel decision and it shows that the extraordinary challenge committees are functioning as intended.

The FTA panels' admirable performance makes them a model for other types of dispute resolution. They provided the inspiration for the creation of the binding arbitration panels established in the 1989 steel consensus agreements, and could serve as a model for reform of the GATT panels.

Chapter 19 Panels

The volume of trade affected by Chapter 19 panels in the first two years is quite large, totalling almost 500 million Canadian dollars.[8] 16 cases have been docketed under Chapter 19, although some have been consolidated and others terminated prior to issuance of a decision. 14 of the cases have been appeals of U.S. Government agency actions; two have been appeals of Canadian Government agency action. There are several reasons why more U.S. decisions have been challenged than Canadian decisions even though there are about the same number of new cases in both countries.[9]

Canadian Studies, Johns Hopkins University, House Comm. on Small Business, 100th Cong., 1st Sess., United States-Canada Free-Trade Agreement 9 (Comm. Print 1987) (discussing the need to resolve disputes "in a quicker fashion" and "in a less expensive way").

8 *See* Appendix One which is available from the authors on request.

9 During the period 1989-1990, the United States initiated two new antidumping cases, Fed. Track Guide to Antidumping Findings and Orders Fed. Track Publications (1991), and three new countervailing duty cases against Canada, Fed. Track Guide to Countervailing Duty Cases, Fed. Track Publications (1991). This compares to four new antidumping cases and no countervailing duty cases brought in Canada against the U.S. during the same period. "International Trade: Use of the GATT Antidumping Code," Report of the U.S. General Accounting Office, GAO/NSIAD-90-238FS (July 1990) at 26 ("GAO Report"). The four antidumping cases involved liquid polyvinyl chloride dispersion, landing nets, transit concrete mixers and small motors. *Id.*

In looking at the panels, four have involved U.S. countervailing duty determinations.[10] The United States uses countervailing duties far more often than Canada,[11] and Canada had no countervailing duty determinations against the United States during the period for which panel review could be sought.

There is an incentive for the government granting the alleged subsidy to challenge the initial determination. A determination of countervailability of a given subsidy program on one product could well affect investigations of other products which might be involved in the same program. If the appeal is successful, it will preclude the use of that subsidy finding against exports of other products.

Concerning antidumping duty determinations, the U.S. system of retrospective review creates an incentive for appeals not present under the Canadian system of prospective duty collection. In somewhat over-simplified terms, the USA requires cash deposits once an antidumping or countervailing duty order has been issued. After collecting the deposits for a year, either party can request a review to determine if the amount of the deposit was correct.[12] Under this system, the importer must make cash deposits, and then go through the review to get the deposits back, even if the dumping has ceased. This creates an incentive to appeal the initial determination; if the challenge is successful, no more deposits need be made, and, as was the case in *Red Raspberries from Canada*,[13] there is a chance to get some of the money back.

By contrast, Canada allows the importation of goods previously found to be dumped without the payment of a deposit or a duty, as long as the prices of the goods have been raised above the "normal value" determined

10 Those four are *Fresh, Chilled or Frozen Pork from Canada*, USA-89-1904-11 (Jan. 30, 1991) (injury); *Fresh, Chilled and Frozen Pork from Canada*, USA-89-1904-06 (March 8, 1991) (subsidies); *New Steel Rails from Canada*, USA-89-1904-09/10 (Aug. 13, 1990) (injury); *New Steel Rails from Canada*, USA-89-1904-07 (Aug. 27, 1990) (subsidies).

11 Horlick, G., and D. Steger, "Subsidies and Countervailing Duties," at note 10, in P. Morici, ed., *Making Free Trade Work: the Canada-U.S. Agreement*, 1990.

12 Horlick, G., "The United States Antidumping System," in J. Jackson, and E. Vermulst, eds., *Antidumping Law and Practice: A Comparative Study*, Michigan: The University of Michigan Press, 1989.

13 USA-89-1904-01 (Dec. 15, 1989).

in the investigation.[14] While the normal value can be changed based on reviews, the new normal value usually applies only to future entries.[15] As a result, most exporters simply raise their prices above the normal value, and pay no duty. Consequently, there is no pool of money to be fought over on review, although there remains the possibility of reducing future duty levels.

Chapter 19 panels have dealt with a heavy load of antidumping and countervailing duty cases quite effectively. The involvement of the Canadian and U.S. governments with Chapter 19 panel review is much less extensive than their involvement with Chapter 18 panels. FTA Article 1904(2) provides for the two governments to request Chapter 19 review and they, in turn, permit private parties to make requests.[16]

The Chapter 19 panels must apply the same test that a reviewing court of the country whose decision is challenged would apply.[17] In the United States, the test is whether the decision is unsupported by substantial evidence on the record, or otherwise not in accordance with laws.[18] In Canada, the test is whether the agency (a) failed to observe a principle of natural justice or otherwise acted beyond or refused to exercise its jurisdiction; (b) erred in law in making its decision or order, whether or not the error appears on the face of the record; or (c) based its decision or order on an erroneous finding of fact that was made in a perverse or capricious manner or without regard to the material before it.[19]

---

14 Magnus, P., "The Canadian Antidumping System," in J. Jackson, and E. Vermulst, eds., *Antidumping Law and Practice: A Comparative* Study, 1989.

15 *Id.*

16 United States-Canada Free-Trade Agreement Implementation Act of 1988, 19 U.S.C. § 2112 note § 408 (1988); Canada-United States Free Trade Agreement Implementation Act, S.C. 1988, c. 65.

17 FTA Article 1904(3).

18 *See* Article 1911 (definition of standard of review), which adopts the standard of Section 516A(b)(1)(B) of the Tariff Act of 1930.

19 *See* Article 1911 (definition of standard of review), which adopts the standard of Section 28(1) of the Federal Court Act.

Both Canada and the United States have adopted procedural rules governing the panel review process.[20] Panel requests must be made within 30 days following the date of publication of the final determination in question.[21] The FTA provides strict deadlines for the review process, usually leading to a final decision within 315 days after a request for panel review.[22] The tight time schedule reflects the FTA's objective of speedy decision making.[23]

Parties submit briefs to the panel, and the panels allow oral argument.[24]

20 *See* Rules of Procedure for Article 1904 Binational Panel Reviews, *Canada Gazette* Part I, 103 (January 14, 1989) as amended *Canada Gazette* Part I, 5398 (Dec. 23, 1989); Rules of Procedure for Article 1904 Binational Panel Reviews, 53 Fed. Reg. 53,212 (Dec. 30, 1988) ("Rules of Procedure").

21 FTA Article 1904(4).

22 FTA Article 1904(14); *see* Appendix 2, Table 1.

23 Binational Panel Reviews and Extraordinary Challenge Committees; United States-Canada Free-Trade Agreement, 53 Fed. Reg. 53,212 (1988); *see also* House Comm. on the Judiciary, United States-Canada Free-Trade Agreement Implementation Act of 1988, H.R. Rep. No. 816, 100th Cong., 2d Sess., pt. 4, at 3 (1988) (the arbitral system's advantages of quickness and low cost will help the parties calculate the economic costs and benefits involved in appealing a case); Testimony of Charles F. Doran, Director, Center of Canadian Studies, Johns Hopkins University, House Comm. on Small Business, 100th Cong., 1st Sess., United States-Canada Free-Trade Agreement 9 (Comm. Print 1987) (discussing the need to resolve disputes "in a quicker fashion" and "in a less expensive way").

24 *See* FTA Article 1904(7). Interestingly, the panel rules only provide for French translation where the case arises from a final determination made in Canada. *See* Rule 28, Rules of Procedure. Participants may use either English or French in any document or oral proceeding, *see* Rule 29, Rules of Procedure, yet an opinion or order of the panel will only be translated (either from English or from French) if the panel determines that the issue is of general interest or importance or the proceedings which led to the order or opinion were conducted in whole or in part in English or French, *see* Rule 30, Rules of Procedure. Oral proceedings will be simultaneously interpreted upon request of a party or if the panel chairman deems that there is a public interest in the panel review. *See* Rule 31, Rules of Procedure.

Chapter 18 Panels

There have been far fewer Chapter 18[25] panels than Chapter 19 panels. Whereas 16 Chapter 19 cases have been docketed, only two Chapter 18 panels have been formed.[26]

Chapter 18 panels operate similarly to Chapter 19 panels, although there are some important distinctions. While the United States and Canada have delegated to private parties the right to request Chapter 19 reviews, only the two national governments can request Chapter 18 reviews.[27] Further, under Chapter 18, the Parties have considerable input into the panel process through the Canada-United States Trade Commission ("Commission").[28] The principal representative of each government on the Commission is the cabinet-level officer or Minister primarily responsible for international trade, or their designees.[29] There is no equivalent to the Commission under Chapter 19.

In contrast to Chapter 19 panels that issue a single binding decision, Chapter 18 panels produce an initial report, which includes recommendations for resolution of the dispute.[30] If the United States or Canada disagrees with the report, it may present a written statement of its

---

25 Chapter 18 panels draw from various elements of Chapter 19 of the Israel-U.S. Free Trade Agreement. Israel-United States Free Trade Agreement, April 22, 1985, U.S.T. ___, T.I.A.S. No. ___, reprinted in 24 I.L.M. 653 (1985). The U.S.-Israel FTA dispute resolution mechanism has been used only once, in a dispute involving machine tools from Israel. "Panel Rules in Favor of Israeli FTA in Machine Tool Dispute Over VRA," 9 *Inside U.S. Trade*, No. 17 at 8 (May 3, 1991). Israel claimed that the United States interfered with the FTA when Taiwan ceased shipments of machine tool components to Israel after the United States counted the completed machine tools against the quota established in the U.S.-Taiwan Machine Tool VRA. *Id.* While the panel's ruling has not yet been made public, it is believed that the panel ruled in favour of Israel. *Id.*

26 Those two cases are: *Canada's Landing Requirements for Pacific Coast Salmon and Herring*, CDA-89-1807-01, (Oct. 16, 1989); *Lobsters from Canada*, USA-89-1807-01 (Dec. 12, 1989).

27 FTA Article 1803.

28 *See* FTA Article 1802(1). For instance, each Chapter 18 panel may establish its own rules of procedure unless the Commission has agreed otherwise. FTA Article 1807(4).

29 FTA Article 1802(2).

30 FTA Article 1807(5).

objections within 14 days after the report is issued.[31] The panel may reconsider the report and issue a final report.[32] The final report is due within 30 days of issuance of the initial report.[33]

Whereas the Chapter 19 panel's decision is binding, and must be enforced absent an extraordinary challenge, the Commission can override a Chapter 18 panel's report.[34] If it does not do so, the panel report, plus any separate opinions and any written views of the Parties, are published unless the Commission agrees otherwise.[35] Upon receipt of the report, the Commission "shall agree" on resolution of the dispute, which "normally" will conform with the panel's recommendation.[36] These provisions give the panel considerable "moral" influence over resolution of the dispute.[37]

While the Chapter 19 panels may only affirm or remand agency decisions, Chapter 18 provides for broader discretion in finding a remedy. The FTA expansively defines potential remedies as the "non-implementation or removal of a measure not conforming with this Agreement or causing nullification or impairment in the sense of Article 2011 or, failing such a resolution, compensation."[38] The FTA does not limit dispute resolution to even these broadly-defined remedies but provides that they are to be used "[w]here possible."[39]

---

31 FTA Article 1807(6).

32 *Id.* The panel may reconsider its report on its own motion, at the request of the Commission, or at the request of either government. *Id.* Reconsideration under Chapter 19 is limited to technical errors. Rule 76, Rules of Procedure for Article 1904 Binational Panel Reviews.

33 *Id.*

34 FTA Article 1807(7) provides that "[u]nless the Commission agrees otherwise," the final report of the panel is to be published. Safeguard decisions by Chapter 18 panels are binding. FTA Article 1806(1).

35 *Id.*

36 FTA Article 1807(8).

37 *Id.*

38 *Id.*

39 *Id.*

Chapter 18 explicitly permits retaliation. FTA Article 1807(9) provides that if the Commission "has not reached agreement or a mutually satisfactory resolution . . . within 30 days of receiving the final report of the panel," a wronged party can "suspend the application to the other party of benefits of equivalent effect until such time as the Parties have reached agreement on a resolution of the dispute."[40]

Both Canada and the United States have adopted model rules for Chapter 18 proceedings.[41]

The Panels are Functioning as Intended by Both Countries

Timeliness of Panel Decisions

FTA dispute resolution is more than twice as fast as U.S. judicial review.[42] Whereas all but two FTA panels have met the FTA's deadline of 315 days (about ten and a half months),[43] judicial review to the Court of International Trade ("CIT") typically takes about 26 months.[44] Even considering the delays in two FTA panels, since some panels have made their decisions before the deadline, the median time for a panel decision is ten and a half months.[45]

---

40 FTA Article 1807(9).

41 *See* Model Rules of Procedures for Chapter 18 Panels, *Canada Gazette* part I, p. 100 (Jan. 14, 1989); Model Rules of Procedures for Chapter 18 Panels, 54 Fed. Reg. 14,372 (April 11, 1989).

42 *See* Appendix Two, Graph "Comparison of Appeal Periods." Canadian judicial review is apparently faster than U.S. judicial review. Administrative Conference of the United States Forum on Binational Dispute Resolution Procedures Under the U.S.-Canada Free Trade Agreement (April 23, 1991) Transcript at 67 (statement of Ms. Holland) ("Administrative Conference Transcript").

43 *See* Appendix Two, Table 1. The failure to meet the deadlines occurred in cases where a panellist had to be replaced.

44 *See* Appendix Two, Table 4. 26 months is the median time for a CIT decision.

45 *See* Appendix Two, Table 1.

The reason the panels issue such prompt decisions is that the FTA provides a tight timetable for filings and oral argument.[46] While the language in the FTA is worded broadly enough to permit a panel to exceed the 315 day deadline,[47] they have not abused this discretion.

The FTA not only provides for quick panel decisions, it also offers speedier remands than the CIT. The median length of time for a first remand to a binational panel is a little over four months[48] compared to six months for a first CIT remand.[49] For a second remand, the median length of time for a binational panel is two and a half months[50] whereas a second remand to the CIT takes five months.[51]

Another reason FTA dispute resolution is faster than judicial review is because FTA decisions are less likely to be reviewed than are CIT decisions. An FTA panel decision can only be challenged by the Canadian or U.S. Government[52] whereas any party can appeal a CIT decision as of right.[53] Further, whereas the Court of Appeals for the Federal Circuit ("CAFC") conducts a *de novo* review,[54] the extraordinary challenge committee's standard of review is very narrow.[55] If a binational panel's decision is challenged, it appears that the time for a decision will be much

---

46 FTA Article 1904(14).

47 FTA Article 1904(14) (emphasis added) states that "rules *shall be designed* to result in final decisions within 315 days of the date in which a request for a panel is made."

48 *See* Appendix Two, Table 2. The median time for the first remand is 130 days. Appendix Two is available from the authors on request.

49 Shambon, "Accomplishing the Legislative Goals for the Court of International Trade: More speed! More speed!" 14 Fordham Int'l L.J. 31 (1990) ("Shambon Article").

50 *See* Appendix Two, Table 2. The median time for a second remand is 77 days.

51 Shambon Article at 19.

52 FTA Article 1904(13).

53 19 U.S.C. § 1516a(9) (1988).

54 *Matsushita Electric Indus. Co., Ltd. v. United States*, 929 F.2d 1577, 1578 (Fed. Cir. 1991); *American Permac, Inc. v. United States*, 831 F.2d 269, 273 (Fed. Cir. 1987) *cert. dismissed*, 485 U.S. 901 (1988).

55 The standard is discussed *infra* at 27.

quicker than for a CAFC decision. While there has only been one extraordinary challenge to date,[56] the entire challenge process took only two and a half months.[57] By comparison, an appeal to the CAFC typically takes over ten months.[58]

Impartiality

Each panel has five members consisting of either three Canadians and two Americans or two Canadians and three Americans.[59]

There was a concern that panels would split along the lines of nationality, whereby panels with a Canadian majority would favour the Canadian position and panels with a U.S. majority would favour the U.S. position. However, this has not occurred. There have been seven cases that resulted in written decisions and in five of those cases, decisions of the Chapter 19 panels have been unanimous.[60]

There is no correlation between the nationality of the panellists and the result. In the *Pork* decision on injury,[61] U.S. panellists sided with Canadian panellists in reaching a unanimous decision against the U.S.

---

56 *Fresh, Chilled or Frozen Pork from Canada*, ECC-91-1904-01USA.

57 *See* Appendix Two, Table 3.

58 *See* Appendix Two, Table 5.

59 Under Chapter 18, each panel must have two Canadian and two U.S. citizens who are appointed by the Government of Canada and the Government of the United States, respectively. The Commission appoints the fifth panellist. If the Commission cannot agree on the fifth panellist, the four appointed panellists may select the fifth panellist. If the four appointed panellists cannot agree, the fifth panellist is selected by lot from the roster of panellists. FTA Article 1807(3).

Under Chapter 19, the two governments select the five panellists in consultation with each other. If they cannot agree on the fifth panellist, the selection procedures are the same as under Chapter 18 except that candidates eliminated by peremptory challenge are excluded from the roster from which the fifth panellist is selected by lot. FTA Annex 1901.2(2), (3).

60 The two decisions that were not unanimous are *New Steel Rails from Canada*, USA-89-1904-09/10 (Review of ITC determination) (one dissent) and *New Steel Rails from Canada*, USA-89-1904-08 (Aug. 30, 1990) (Review of ITA determination) (one dissent).

61 USA-89-1904-11.

International Trade Commission ("ITC"). In *Raspberries*,[62] two U.S. panellists sided with the Canadian majority against the U.S. Department of Commerce ("Commerce"). Conversely, in *New Steel Rails*,[63] the panel had a Canadian majority but it supported the position of the ITC. In that case, the ITC found that Canadian rails did not presently injure U.S. rail producers, but that they threatened to do so in the future. The ITC's affirmative decision was based on a three-three split,[64] so it was the weakest possible agency decision. Even so, the Canadian majority panel gave great deference to the three-commissioner ITC "plurality" and upheld the decision.[65]

The results of the Chapter 18 panels have been different. There have been only two panels, one with a Canadian majority, the other with a U.S. majority. Both decisions were resolved in favour of the United States. However, the panellists in *Lobsters* split on national lines. In *Salmon*, some panellists dissented on certain issues but it is unclear from the opinion whether the panellists' decisions correlate with nationality.

Quality of Decisions

Commentators agree that the quality of FTA panel decisions is quite good. Professor Andreas F. Lowenfeld undertook an in-depth analysis of panel decisions under the FTA. He concluded:

> [T]he consideration given by panel members to the issues and the contentions of the parties has been careful, and . . . the opinions have been well thought through and well crafted. Though no one can be expected to agree with all of the opinions in every detail . . ., as a whole the opinions are of high quality, and should leave even losing parties--including the government

---

62 USA-89-1904-01.

63 USA-89-1904-09/10.

64 Tie votes by the ITC in U.S. AD/CVD cases are resolved in favour of the U.S. petitioning industry. 19 U.S.C. § 1677(ii) (1988).

65 One of the three Canadian panellists dissented. *New Steel Rails from Canada*, USA-89-1904-09/10 at 95.

agencies concerned--confident that they received a full and fair hearing.[66]

The Commerce Department's legal advisor for the U.S. Secretariat also commented on the high quality of panel decisions at a recent forum.[67] She noted that "consensus reigns among . . . both private participants and [those] in government, that panel decisions are of a relatively high caliber compared to CIT decisions."[68]

At oral argument, the panellists have generally been knowledgeable and well-prepared.[69] Overall, the Canadian panellists have adeptly grasped U.S. trade law issues and shown no hesitancy in quizzing counsel on their positions. The questions of U.S. panellists have reflected their "informed experience."[70]

Administrative Feasibility

The administrative functioning of the dispute panels has been remarkably smooth.

The panellist selection process is handled by the Office of the United States Trade Representative ("USTR") and the Canadian Ministry of International Trade ("Ministry"). Within 30 days of a request for panel review, the United States and Canada must each appoint two panellists.[71]

In the United States, USTR reviews the roster and eliminates candidates with potential conflicts. USTR then instructs the U.S. Secretariat to contact candidates selected by USTR to determine availability and any conflicts of

---

66 Lowenfeld, "Binational Dispute Settlement Under Chapters 18 and 19 of the Canada-United States Free Trade Agreement: An Interim Appraisal" (Dec. 1990) (report prepared for the consideration of the Administrative Conference of the United States).

67 Administrative Conference Transcript at 56 (statement of Ms. Koteen).

68 *Id.*

69 Ince and Sherman, "Binational Panel Reviews under Article 19 of the U.S.-Canada Free Trade Agreement: A Novel Approach to International Dispute Resolution," *Federal Bar News & Journal* at 139 (March-April 1990).

70 *Id.*

71 FTA Annex 1901.2(2).

interest.[72] The Secretariat reports the results of its search to USTR which makes the final selection of panellists.

In Canada, the panellist selection process is initiated by the Canadian Secretariat. The Secretariat provides *all* roster members with detailed lists of interested parties (to determine conflicts of interest) and a timetable. Interested roster members submit a statement of availability to the Secretariat who compiles a list of potential panellists which is forwarded to the Ministry. The Canadian Members of Panels Regulations provide that a board chaired by the Minister of International Trade and consisting of the Minister of Finance and other members designated by the Prime Minister appoints panellists.[73]

Each country is allowed four peremptory challenges to be exercised simultaneously and in confidence.[74] Officials from the Canadian and U.S. governments confirm that peremptory challenges are frequently exercised by both governments mainly on the grounds of conflict of interest -- although a government need not provide a reason for its challenge. The fifth panellist is jointly chosen by both countries.[75] If the countries cannot agree on a fifth panellist, the four previously selected panellists choose the fifth panellist from the roster.[76] If the panellists cannot agree, the fifth panellist is chosen by lot from the roster.[77]

By all reports, the process of selecting the fifth panellist has been fairly amicable. An informal practice has evolved whereby the nationality of the fifth panellist alternates between an American and a Canadian. To date, there have been no reported challenges to panellists by parties to the proceedings.

Both the United States and Canada have established Secretariats pursuant to FTA Article 1909. The Secretariats receive and file all requests, briefs

---

72 All potential panellists (Canadian and U.S.) must submit a statement disclosing conflicts of interest.

73 *Canada Gazette* Part II, 134 (June 1, 1989).

74 *Id.*

75 FTA, Annex 1901.2(3).

76 *Id.*

77 *Id.*

and other papers.[78] They assist the panel members in coordinating schedules and making the necessary arrangements for hearings. They have been extremely helpful in providing guidance to the parties concerning panel rules and procedures.

Binding Effect

Not all decisions of Chapter 18 panels are binding, whereas by the terms of the FTA every Chapter 19 decision is binding.[79] Article 1904(9) provides: "The decision of a panel under this Article shall be binding on the Parties with respect to the particular matter between the Parties that is before the panel."

The binding effect of a panel's decision has been tested twice already. In the very first case appealed to a Chapter 19 panel, *Red Raspberries from Canada*,[80] the panel analyzed the Commerce methodology for calculating a dumping margin. As the panel observed, under 19 U.S.C. § 1677b(a), Commerce can calculate a dumping margin by comparing U.S. sales to, in order of priority, home market sales, third country sales and constructed value.[81] Commerce did not use home market sales.[82] The panel held defective and remanded Commerce's findings that the home market sales of the two companies were inadequate to use as a basis for foreign market value.[83] On remand, Commerce simply gave a better explanation for its decision.[84] The parties again asked for panel review and, this time, the panel directed Commerce to use home market sales as a basis for

---

78 FTA Article 1909(9).

79 FTA Article 1806(1) provides that reviews of safeguard actions are binding and that Canada and the United States may agree to make other Chapter 18 reviews binding.

80 USA-89-1904-01.

81 *Id.* at 15-16.

82 *Id.* at 2.

83 *Id.* at 25.

84 Department of Commerce Determination on Remand, *Red Raspberries from Canada*, USA-89-1904-01 (January 26, 1990).

comparison.[85] On the second remand, Commerce complied with the panel's directive and calculated the margins based on the home market prices of the two companies.[86] The dumping margins vanished. The panel was able to change the result of the case because the U.S. Government was bound by the panel's decision.

The second occasion on which the binding nature of the panel's decision was tested involved *Fresh, Chilled or Frozen Pork from Canada.*[87] In that case, the panel reviewed the U.S. International Trade Commission's decision that the U.S. industry was threatened with material injury by reason of subsidized pork imports from Canada.[88] The panel found that several of the ITC's findings "rely heavily or flow directly from faulty use of statistics."[89] It remanded for the ITC to reconsider its findings.[90]

The ITC, realizing the weakness of its position on remand, reopened the record.[91] It attempted to strengthen the basis for its findings and then reissued the same decision.[92] The Canadian parties asked the panel to consider the ITC's decision on remand and the panel did so.[93] This time, the panel was extremely explicit. It noted that "the ITC's record has been combed not once but twice in the search for substantial evidence of material

85 *Red Raspberries from Canada*, USA-89-1904-01.

86 *Red Raspberries from Canada*, 55 Fed. Reg. 28,074 (Dep't Comm. 1990).

87 USA-89-1904-11.

88 *See id.* at 16.

89 Id.

90 *Id.* Specifically, the panel stated "that the ITC's findings on the nature of Canadian subsidies, the likelihood of increased Canadian pork exports, the likelihood of an increase in market penetration ratios, price suppression, distribution channels, the imminence of threat of material injury due to the countercyclical nature of the pork cycle and the vulnerability of the U.S. domestic industry are all colored by the questionable finding of greatly increased Canadian pork production."

91 55 Fed. Reg. 39,073 (Int'l Trade Comm. 1990).

92 Fresh, Chilled, or Frozen Pork from Canada, Inv. No. 701-TA-298, USITC Pub. 2330 (Oct. 1990).

93 *Fresh, Chilled or Frozen Pork from Canada (Injury)*, USA-89-1904-11 at 3-4.

injury. "[94] It found none, stating "that the majority Commissioners' findings of a threat of imminent material injury are not supported by substantial evidence."[95] The ITC then reversed its finding of threat of injury, declaring that it was required to do so by the panel's directive.[96]

Although the ITC reversal in the *Pork* case indicates that the U.S. Government honoured its commitment under FTA Article 1904.9 to be bound by the decisions of Chapter 19 panels, its statements and actions suggest that it was doing so reluctantly. In the majority opinion on Second Remand, Commissioners Rohr and Newquist repeatedly criticized the panel's decision and warned that the decision would not impact their future practice.[97] The U.S. Government, at the urging of the ITC, requested an extraordinary challenge committee to review the binational panel's Second Remand to the ITC. The committee upheld the binational panel decision. The United States then revoked the countervailing duty order and refunded the duties deposited.[98]

The ECC is Functioning as Predicted

FTA Article 1904.13 allows a Party to challenge the decision of a binational panel in the following limited circumstances:
1. a) a member of the panel was guilty of gross misconduct, bias, or a serious conflict of interest, or otherwise materially violated the rules of conduct,
    b) the panel seriously departed from a fundamental rule of procedure, *or*

---

94 *Id.* at 7.

95 *Id.* at 37.

96 Fresh, Chilled or Frozen Pork from Canada: Second Remand, Inv. No. 701-TA-298, USITC Pub. 2362 (Feb. 1991).

97 *Id.* at 3, 5, 16, 34.

98 56 Fed. Reg. 29,464 (Dep't Comm. 1991). A separate Chapter 19 Panel had overruled the FTA on several aspects of the subsidy finding, but the revocation of the order made further compliance unnecessary.

c) the panel manifestly exceeded its powers, authority or jurisdiction set forth in this Article.[99]

In addition, the Party must show that the situation is so serious that at least one of the actions in subparagraph (a) materially affected the panel's decision *and* poses a continued threat to the integrity of the binational panel review process should the decision be allowed to stand.[100] If an extraordinary challenge committee ("ECC") finds that the narrow grounds for an extraordinary challenge have been established, the ECC may vacate or remand the binational panel decision.[101]

The drafters of the extraordinary challenge process expected that it would be used infrequently,[102] and, in fact, it has been invoked in only one case: *Fresh, Chilled and Frozen Pork from Canada*.[103] The committee's decision makes it likely that challenges will be infrequent.

On March 29, 1991, the Government of the United States, at the urging of the petitioner, requested the formation of an ECC to review the issues raised by the Panel's second remand decision.[104] The ECC consists of two retired Canadian justices and one retired United States judge.[105] Although FTA Annex 1904.13(2) provides that decisions should typically be rendered within 30 days, the ECC announced that it would require 60 days to make its decision. It also arranged to hear oral arguments in the case although FTA Annex 1904.13 contains no express provision for oral argument.

Those challenging the panel's decision argued, *inter alia*, that the panel failed to apply U.S. law because it relied on FTA--rather than U.S.-- principles of due process and issued a more restrictive remand than would

99 FTA Article 1904.13, (emphasis added).

100 FTA Article 1904.13(b).

101 FTA Annex 1904.13.

102 Testimony of M. Jean Anderson, Chief Counsel for International Trade, U.S. Dept. of Commerce Subcommittee on Courts, Civil Liberties and the Administration of Justice of the Committee on the Judiciary, U.S. House of Representatives, 100th Cong., 2d Sess. 69, 75-76 (1988).

103 ECC-91-1904-01USA (June 14, 1991).

104 "Request for an Extraordinary Challenge Committee" (March 29, 1991).

105 Sitting U.S. judges cannot serve as arbitrators, so retired judges sit on the ECCs. Code of Judicial Conduct Canon 4 F (1991).

be allowed under U.S. law.[106] Respondents argued that the panel correctly applied the FTA and U.S. law, and that the panel review process will be threatened if appeals become politicized and routine.[107]

Political pressure played a major role in the *Pork* case because the deadline for USTR's decision to invoke the ECC process fell at the same time Congress was deciding whether to extend fast track legislation[108] for an additional two years. In light of its ambitious trade agenda, including the North American Free Trade Agreement and Uruguay Round negotiations, the Administration was anxious for Congress to extend fast track authority. The NPPC filed its petition urging an extraordinary challenge on March 11, 1991, and between March 11 and March 29 United States Trade Representative Carla Hills received a series of multiple signature letters from approximately 90 members of Congress encouraging her to request an ECC.[109] The implicit message of the letters was that support for fast track extension was dependent on a request for an ECC. Although Ambassador Hills had stated at a House Agriculture Hearing on March 13, 1991 her belief that the extraordinary challenge procedure was aimed at improprieties,[110] she succumbed to the political pressure (specifically, a promise of three Senate votes in favour of fast track) on March 29, 1991 and requested formation of an ECC based on the less serious ground of failure to correctly apply United States law.

106 *See* ITC Brief at 58; NPPC Brief at 34.

107 Brief of the Government of Canada, *Fresh, Chilled or Frozen Pork from Canada*, ECC-91-1904-01USA (April 19, 1991) at 57 ("Brief of the Gov't of Canada").

108 Under the United States Constitution, the President of the United States has the power to negotiate trade agreements, but Congressional legislation is required to implement them. Congress's power of amendment encourages special interest groups to tinker with negotiated treaties and thereby undermines the President's credibility at the bargaining table, Congress approved, in the Trade Act of 1974, an alternative method of approval: the fast-track process. With fast-track the House and Senate have limited periods of time during which they may approve or reject legislation implementing a negotiated trade agreement. The legislation cannot be amended. 19 U.S.C. § 2191 (1988).

109 Brief of the Gov't of Canada at 11.

110 *See* Hearing on Fast Track Trade Negotiation Authority before the House Committee on Agriculture, 102d Cong., 1st Sess. (March 13, 1991) (statement of Ambassador Carla Hills, United States Trade Representative).

On June 14, 1991, the EEC issued a unanimous decision in favour of the Canadian interests.[111] In doing so, the committee upheld the binational panel's decision. The panel had found that a decision by the U.S. International Trade Commission ("ITC") was unsupported.[112] As a consequence of the committee's ruling, countervailing duties on Canadian pork imports must be refunded and no further duties can be imposed.

The committee's decision strengthens the FTA's binational panel review process. The committee emphasized the extremely narrow three-prong standard of review for challenges.[113] It stated that the three-prong requirement "provides explicit, narrow grounds for extraordinary challenges and makes clear that an extraordinary challenge is not intended to function as a routine appeal."[114] The committee noted that words "such as 'gross,' 'serious,' 'fundamental,' 'materially,' 'manifestly,' and 'threatens,' which appear in the statute, highlight the committee's formidable standard of review.[115] Further, the committee opined that an ECC was not like an appellate court[116] and that the short 30-day "typical" period for a challenge makes it "clear that a committee is not intended to conduct an in-depth review regarding the merits of the investigation within such a short timeframe."[117]

The committee came close to reprimanding the United States Trade Representative for bringing the challenge. The committee dismissed the challenge, stating that "the allegations do not meet the threshold for an extraordinary challenge."[118]

---

111 Fresh, Chilled or Frozen Pork from Canada, ECC-91-1904-01USA (June 14, 1991) ("ECC Pork Decision").

112 *See Supra* at 25.

113 ECC Pork Decision at 9-10.

114 *Id.* at 10. (Citing statement of Administrative Action, United States-Canada Free Trade Agreement at 116, *reprinted in* H.R. Doc. No. 216, 100th Cong., 2d Sess., 163, 278 (1988).)

115 *Id.* at 11.

116 *Id.* at 12.

117 *Id.* at 13.

118 *Id.* at 3.

The committee's decision also clarifies that binational panels have broad authority. The ITC had argued that the panels could only give open-ended remands and that the panel went too far in creating a rule of finality.[119] The committee disagreed. It held that "there are no restrictions on the Panel's power to remand with or without instructions to the competent investigating authority."[120] By upholding the panel's authority to limit remands, the committee recognized the FTA's goals of speedy and inexpensive review, which it cited in the decision. *Id.* at 16.

In sum, the committee's decision should have the effect of making challenges to panel decisions very infrequent. The challenge process is functioning as intended by both countries.

Use of FTA Dispute Resolution Panels as a Model for Other Negotiations

The FTA binational panels have been one of the most successful elements of the FTA. They already have served as an impetus for other agreements, specifically the steel consensus agreements of 1989. It is possible that some elements of the panels could be adopted by the GATT.

Steel Consensus Arrangements of 1989

In 1989, the United States entered into steel consensus agreements with the major exporters of steel to the United States.[121] The purpose of the agreements was to eliminate or restrict subsidies and reduce both tariff and nontariff barriers affecting steel trade. As part of each of those agreements there is a dispute settlement agreement that draws on the FTA panels (as well as the World Bank's International Centre for the Settlement of Investment Disputes) as a model.

---

119 The ITC and the petitioner both argued that an infinite number of remands are required. Brief of the International Trade Commission, *Fresh, Chilled or Frozen Pork from Canada*, ECC-91-1904-01USA at 72 (April 19, 1991) ("ITC Brief"); *see also* Brief of the National Pork Producers Council, *Fresh, Chilled or Frozen Pork from Canada*, ECC-91-1904-01USA at 32 (April 19, 1991) ("NPPC Brief").

120 ECC Pork decision at 19.

121 Specifically, the United States concluded steel agreements with the European Communities, the Republic of Korea, Mexico, Brazil, Australia, Japan, Trinidad and Tobago, Austria, Finland, Czechoslovakia, Hungary, Poland, Rumania, Yugoslavia, Venezuela, Sweden and the Peoples Republic of China.

The steel consensus agreements all adopt the basic dispute resolution structure of the FTA panels. It is useful to compare the USA-European Economic Community Consensus Agreement ("USA-EC Agreement"), which is typical of the steel consensus arrangements, with the FTA.

The USA-EC Agreement mirrors the FTA in establishing firm dates by which various types of action must occur. The time period for the USA and EC to settle a dispute under the agreement by consultation is 15 days compared to the 30 days allowed by Chapter 18.[122] Thereafter, as under Chapter 18, either party can refer a matter to arbitration and appoint an arbitrator.[123] The other party then has 15 days to appoint its arbitrator. Thus, within 15 days of the request for arbitration, two of the three arbitrators are appointed. Similarly, under Chapter 18, four of the five panellists are appointed by day 15.[124] In contrast, Chapter 19 of the FTA provides for the appointment of four panellists within 30 days.[125]

The length of time for selection of the third arbitrator is shorter than for the selection of the fifth FTA panellist. The two arbitrators have 15 days to appoint a third arbitrator,[126] whereas under Chapter 19 of the FTA Parties have an additional 25 days to select the fifth panellist,[127] and under Chapter 18 of the FTA, if the Parties fail to agree on the fifth panellist, the other panellists must select the fifth panellist within 30 days of the establishment of the panel.[128]

The USA-EC Agreement follows Chapter 19 of the FTA in providing for a random selection process in the event there is no agreement on the swing vote arbitrator.[129]

---

122 FTA Article 1807(1).

123 *Compare* U.S.-EC Agreement Article 5(2) *with* FTA Article 1807(2).

124 FTA Article 1807(3).

125 FTA Annex 1901.2(2).

126 U.S.-EC Agreement Article 5(2).

127 FTA Annex 1901.2(3).

128 FTA Article 1807(3).

129 U.S.-EC Agreement, Article 5; FTA Annex 1901.2(3).

One important distinction between the FTA and the USA-EC Agreement is that under the former, the swing vote is a national of either Canada or the United States[130] whereas under the latter, the swing vote is not a national of either party.[131]

Both the FTA and the USA-EC Agreement provide that the panellists (or arbitrators) cannot "take instructions" from either Party.[132] While the FTA merely points out that the panellists shall be objective, the USA-EC Agreement goes a step further and specifies that the arbitrators "shall not have a financial interest in the dispute."[133] However, the FTA does provide for the establishment of a code of conduct,[134] and that code provides that a panellist shall not have a financial interest in the case.[135]

The USA-EC Agreement follows Chapter 18 of the FTA in the method for appointing a chairman. The USA-EC Agreement provides that the neutral person shall be the chairman.[136] The FTA provides in Chapter 18 that the fifth panellist shall chair the panel.[137] In contrast, Chapter 19 of the FTA provides that the panellists shall elect a chairman from among the lawyers on the panel.[138]

While Chapter 19 of the FTA provides that a majority of the panellists on each panel shall be lawyers,[139] the USA-EC Agreement mirrors

---

130 The fifth panellist is selected from the roster of panellists. Annex 1901.2(1). Each of the candidates on the roster must be a citizen of Canada or the United States. *Id.*

131 U.S.-EC Agreement, Article 5.

132 FTA Article 1807(1); FTA Annex 1901.2(1); U.S.-EC Agreement, Article 5(2).

133 *Id.*

134 FTA Article 1910 Annex 1901.2(6).

135 Code of Conduct for Proceedings Under Chapters 18 and 19 of the United States-Canada Free-Trade Agreement, 54 Fed. Reg. 14,371 (April 11, 1989); *Canada Gazette*, Part I, 96 (Jan. 14, 1989).

136 U.S.-EC Agreement, Article 5.

137 FTA Article 1807(4).

138 FTA Annex 1901.2(4).

139 FTA Annex 1901.2(2).

Chapter 18 of the FTA and does not specify that any arbitrators need be lawyers. Since Chapter 18 panellists and the USA-EC Arrangement arbitrators do not have to deal with the complicated antidumping and countervailing duty laws, they may have less of a need for a legal background than Chapter 19 panellists.[140]

The USA-EC Agreement also follows the FTA in that it provides for the establishment of rules of procedure.[141] Similarly, both the USA-EC Agreement and the FTA provide for written submissions and oral argument.[142] The USA-EC Agreement follows Chapter 18 in leaving the timeframe for written submissions and oral argument to the rules of procedure.[143] In contrast, Chapter 19 sets explicit guidelines.[144]

The USA-EC Agreement does not follow the FTA concerning costs associated with the panels. Chapter 19 of the FTA provides that the costs of panellists are to be borne equally by the Parties,[145] and Chapter 18 is silent as the costs. However, the USA-EC Agreement provides that each party shall bear the cost of its own arbitrator and the parties will split the Chairman's costs and remaining costs.[146] The FTA's approach seems more even-handed. By providing that the costs are divided equally for all panellists, the FTA makes it less likely that one panellist considers himself a U.S. panellist and more likely that he considers himself a panellist for the

---

140 Interestingly, none of the present ITC commissioners, whose decisions the Chapter 19 panellists examine, are lawyers. (However, the nominees for two vacancies on the ITC are both lawyers).

141 U.S.-EC Agreement, Article 5; FTA Article 1807(4); FTA Article 1904(14).

142 U.S.-EC Agreement, Article 5; FTA Article 1807(4); FTA Article 1904(14).

143 U.S.-EC Agreement, Article 5; FTA Article 1807(4).

144 FTA Article 1904(14).

145 FTA Annex 1901.2(13).

146 U.S.-EC Agreement, Article 5.

Parties.[147] In any event, one party should not be allowed to pay "its" arbitrator more than the other party.

The USA-EC Agreement, like Chapter 19 of the FTA, provides a deadline for the decision and provides that decisions are to be made by majority vote.[148] Only Chapter 18 specifies that panellists may furnish separate opinions on matters not unanimously agreed.[149] The deadline for the arbitrators' decision (three months from the appointment of the chairman), is identical for the USA-EC Agreement and Chapter 18 of the FTA.[150] This deadline is much shorter than that for the panellists' decision under Chapter 19 (315 days after the request for panel review is filed).[151]

The USA-EC Agreement provides for a preliminary remedy to offset the effects of a violation of the agreement.[152] Similarly, Chapter 18 provides for the issuance of an initial report.[153]

Both the USA-EC Agreement and Chapter 19 of the FTA provide that the panel's decision shall be binding.[154] However, the USA-EC Agreement, like Chapter 18, provides for situations where the parties do not implement the panel's decision. The USA-EC Arrangement provides that if the United States or USA-EC fails to implement the panel's decision and the two governments are unable to agree on appropriate compensation or other remedial action, "then the other party may propose to the panel suspension

147 In addition, since most Chapter 19 panels have been convened in the United States, requiring each Party to bear expenses for its selections could disadvantage Canada. Its panellists have to travel to Washington, DC whereas most of the U.S. panellists reside in the Washington, DC area.

148 U.S.-EC Agreement, Article 5 (3-4); FTA Article 1904(14), Annex 1901.2(5).

149 FTA Article 1807(5).

150 *Compare* U.S.-EC Agreement, Article 5(4) *with* FTA Article 1807(5).

151 The U.S.-EC Agreement permits the 30-day deadline to be extended if "extraordinary circumstances" prevent the panel from meeting the deadline. U.S.-EC Agreement, Article 5.

152 U.S.-EC Agreement, Article 5.

153 FTA Article 1807(6).

154 FTA Article 1904(9); U.S.-EC Agreement, Article 5(7).

of equivalent benefits under the Agreement to the non-complying party."[155] Likewise, Chapter 18 provides that if the matter is not satisfactorily resolved, a Party "shall be free to suspend the application to the other Party of benefits of equivalent effect until such time as the Parties have reached Agreement on a resolution of the dispute."[156] Thus, under both the USA-EC Agreement and Chapter 18, if the parties do not implement the panel's decision, they can agree on compensation or some other remedy. If this fails, the injured party can retaliate.[157]

GATT

GATT panel dispute resolution could be improved by incorporating some aspects of FTA panels into the GATT system.

One of the past criticisms of GATT dispute resolution was that the process is too lengthy. The Montreal Understanding of 1989[158] provided firm deadlines, but proceedings can still be longer than under Chapter 19. GATT could adopt time limits such as those in the FTA to cure the problem.

A major weaknesses of the GATT panels is that a country can block the decision.[159] The FTA panels have shown that countries have not ceded their sovereignty and suffered dreadful consequences by agreeing to be bound by the panel's decision. GATT members, too, could agree to give binding effect in a timely manner to panel decisions.[160]

155 *Id.*

156 FTA Article 1807(9).

157 *Id.*

158 36 BISD 61 (1990).

159 See, e.g., *Canada-Imposition of Countervailing Duties on Inputs of Manufacturing Beef from the EEC* (Oct. 13, 1987) (blocked by the Gov't of Canada); *United States: Definition of Industry Concerning Wine and Grape Products* (March 24, 1986) (blocked by the United States).

160 See *Draft Final Act Embodying the Results of the Uruguay Round of Multilateral Trade Negotiations,* MTN.TNC/W/35 at 296-97 (Nov. 26, 1990).

Conclusions

The FTA panels have been performing well. They have issued timely, well-crafted, and impartial decisions. The panellist selection process has been amicable, and the Parties have given the panel decisions binding effect. The ECC process is working well. There has been only one challenge, and the decision in that case (upholding the panel's decision) establishes that challenges should be infrequent.

The efficiency of the FTA panels is widely acknowledged in the international legal community. They have already served as an inspiration for other agreements. They also provide useful precedents for reform of the GATT dispute resolution processes.[161]

---

161 Appendices detailing the research on how we calculated the time periods for court and dispute panel cases are available from the authors upon request.

Chapter 2

The Canada-USA Free Trade Agreement: Issues of Process

Judith H. Bello and Gilbert R. Winham

Introduction

On September 26, 1985, Prime Minister Brian Mulroney of Canada proposed that the United States enter into a negotiation for a bilateral free trade agreement between the two countries. The U.S. Government accepted this proposal, although congressional approval for the negotiation was only granted by the narrowest of margins. On October 3, 1987, a long and sometimes difficult negotiation was concluded with the signing of an Elements of Agreement, which was converted into a formal agreement by December 11 of that year. In the United States, Congressional approval for the Free Trade Agreement (FTA) occurred without substantial difficulty, but Canadian acceptance of the FTA was effectively postponed until the Mulroney Government won a new mandate in the bitterly-fought election during the autumn of 1988.

This paper will examine important elements of the negotiation process in both countries. In the United States, this will include the politics of the grant by Congress of fast track negotiating authority, and the formal and informal roles of the private sector interest groups. In Canada, interest groups will also be examined, as well as the management of Federal-provincial relations, role and effect of the media, and the impact of public opinion.

Review of the Negotiation Process

Negotiation of the FTA took place in five stages; see table 1. The *first stage* consisted of a series of exploratory meetings during which various issues were placed on the table and work groups were formed. This stage revealed differences in the two parties' approaches to the negotiation. Canada based its approach on the principle of "national treatment," which would have swept away tariffs and most other restrictions on trade, such as quotas and protectionist government procurement policies. A national treatment approach was also designed to modify cross-border trade laws substantially.[1] By comparison, the United States had no equivalent grand plan for the negotiation. It viewed the negotiation more as an opportunity to expand and strengthen the GATT bilaterally than as a new economic constitution between the two North American partners. The United States pursued what was known as the "irritants approach," which was to use the negotiation to get the Canadian Government to change a number of trade-related practices that had led to friction between the two countries.

By the end of the first phase, most major issues had been looked at, and groups were formed to carry out the technical and analytical work needed to support the negotiation. Much of the work was a matter of determining constituents' positions on the various issues. For example, a preparatory meeting of representatives from industries that had complained about Canadian practices regarding the protection of intellectual property (namely, pharmaceutical and software industries) revealed that these groups were generally unenthusiastic about being included in a freer trade agreement with Canada. Some group members felt they could get a better deal by negotiating directly with the Canadian Government. Similarly, on government procurement, the early working group meetings received indications that the General Service Administration was opposed to a bilateral procurement agreement with Canada. Since the U.S. procurement market was ten times the size of Canada's, U.S. negotiators argued that an agreement in this area would not produce equivalent concessions.

The *second stage* of the negotiation, which consisted of 17 formal bargaining sessions, lasted from mid-November 1986 to the breakdown of

---

1   For example, the national treatment approach as pursued by Canada would have involved dropping antidumping procedures entirely between that country and the United States. Both countries would then have been obliged to rely on existing domestic measures such as competition and antitrust policies to ensure that trade was conducted fairly across the border.

Table 1
Canada-USA Free Trade Negotiations
Negotiating Stages

Stage	Duration	Activity
First	May 21, 1986-Sept. 28, 1986	Preliminary meetings (five); working groups formed.
Second	Nov. 12, 1986-Sept. 23, 1987	Negotiation sessions (17); Canada terminates negotiation.
Third	Sept. 28, 1987-Oct. 3, 1987	Meetings of ministers and advisers; ad referendum agreement concluded.
Fourth	Oct. 4, 1987-Dec. 11, 1987	Legal drafting of final agreement; some further negotiation.
Fifth	Jan. 2, 1988-Nov. 21, 1988	Legislative implementation; election in Canada.

talks on September 23, 1987. These largely technical meetings were conducted mainly by the respective specialists from both countries' bureaucracies. Generally the negotiators needed to get some form of political mandate to tackle their particular subject, then they would proceed to negotiate through initiatives and responses. For example, after an economic impact study was conducted by the U.S. International Trade Commission in January 1987, the two sides began earnest negotiations on the elimination of each others' tariffs. Each side made proposals about which products should benefit from immediate, medium term, and longer-term tariff elimination, and responded to proposals made by the other side. On services, the United States tabled a comprehensive proposal that was designed to make the right to "market access" a part of the Free Trade Agreement. Canada resisted this concept early in the negotiation.

The Canadian press covered the entire negotiation in considerable detail, which generated some notoriety for senior negotiators and promoted debate on sensitive issues. For example, there was strong opposition in Canada to including the Canada-USA automotive agreement in the negotiation, and hence the Canadian Government often proclaimed the agreement was not on the table even while it was effectively negotiating issues of auto trade. Another example was culture, on which Americans and Canadians disagreed sharply, and which the press often managed to turn into a source of misunderstanding and manipulation throughout the negotiation.

Throughout the negotiation the differences in the political seniority of the two negotiating teams created problems for the negotiation. In Canada's view, access to senior officials was assured on the Canadian side but not on the American side, thus creating a perception of imbalance that ultimately left the Canadian side unwilling to continue the negotiation. Throughout the negotiation, a common Canadian tactic had been to elevate issues to a political level wherever possible. Canada took advantage of summit meetings between President Reagan and Prime Minister Mulroney, as well as the Venice Economic Summit in June 1987, to press its case for dispute settlement and other issues.

On September 23, 1987, at the 22nd meeting of the two negotiating teams, the Canadian delegation announced that the United States was "not responding on elements fundamental to Canada's position" and suspended the talks. Much had been accomplished up to that point, including a nearly complete reduction on tariffs, and preliminary drafting of agreements in other areas such as agriculture, services, investment, and energy. However, Canada continued to press the United States for a "binding" mechanism that would circumvent U.S. trade remedies, while the United States demanded commitments from Canada limiting the use of subsidies that went well beyond the standard in existing U.S. trade laws. The result was a standoff and a breakdown of the negotiation.

The *third stage* of the negotiation, which was precipitated by the Canadian walkout, lasted from Wednesday, September 23, to Sunday, October 4. The immediate effect of the walkout was to raise the level of negotiation. Since this had been an objective of Canada for some time, it led some Americans to view the Canadian move as being driven more by tactics than substance. It also led to criticism from some in Congress, who felt less able to control senior administration officials than the career trade officials who had largely been carrying the negotiation.

On the U.S. side, responsibility for the negotiation was quickly assumed by Treasury Secretary James Baker, chairman of the Cabinet Economic Policy Council, and U.S. Trade Representative Clayton Yeutter. In Canada, the negotiation was effectively managed from the Prime Minister's office, under the direction of Derek Burney, Chief of Staff, and conducted by Trade Minister Pat Carney and Finance Minister Michael Wilson. Treasury Secretary Baker initiated an urgent round of consultations and analyses on September 23. The Americans quickly concluded that an agreement would meet important U.S. objectives. Even more importantly, they realized that a failure would be a damaging blow to the Administration. Further, they concluded that there was enough room for manoeuvring to make agreement possible; for example, Canada was already demonstrating flexibility in downgrading its rhetoric surrounding the dispute settlement issue from "binding" and "definitive" to "objective and impartial."

On Saturday, September 26, Prime Minister Mulroney received a new proposal from the United States regarding joint rules that would modify national laws on subsidies and dumping. This triggered a set of urgent negotiations by meetings and telephone calls the following week. The negotiators were, however, unable to break the deadlock on subsidies, and the FTA appeared doomed. Then, at mid-week, Baker met with the Senate Finance Committee. In a surprising turn of events spearheaded by Senator Bill Bradley (D-N.J.) and based on a concept pioneered by Rep. Sam Gibbons (D-Fl.), Chairman of the International Trade Subcommittee of the House Committee on Ways and Means, several committee members subsequently supported a different approach to the negotiation. Both sides were to postpone substantive amendments to national antidump (AD) and countervail (CVD) laws until some future date. Meanwhile, the trade remedy legislation in both countries would remain intact. The United States would agree to an ad hoc binational panel review process, but until new rules were established the panels would operate on the basis of each country's domestic antidumping and countervailing duty legislation. The main power of the panels would be that of judicial-like review over antidumping and countervail cases.

The new approach provided the basis for a final marathon session in Washington on October 2-4. With both technical and political personnel in attendance, the deal came together very quickly. The focus continued to be dispute settlement; but in key areas such as investment, financial services, culture, and alcoholic beverages, both parties exchanged concessions they had withheld until the last minute. With virtually the entire agreement concluded, attention then turned back to the last outstanding issue, the operation of the binational tribunal.

The last demand of the Canadians was assurance that Congress would not be able to revoke a decision of the binational tribunal. For the Americans, the demand appeared impossible to meet; Congress is constitutionally empowered to regulate foreign commerce, and the agreement with Canada could not bind future Congresses. For the Canadians, however, the demand was a deal-breaker; without it, there was no agreement. What both sides finally accepted was a U.S. commitment that future amendments to antidumping or countervail laws that affected goods from the other country would be required to name that party in the amending legislation. Furthermore, future statutory amendments were to be subject to binational panels that would have the right to issue declaratory opinions whether challenged amendments were consistent with the FTA. Resolution of this issue essentially completed the FTA negotiation, which was recorded in a document entitled "Elements of the Agreement."

The *fourth stage* of the negotiation, which went from October 5 to December 11, 1987, entailed turning the "Elements of Agreement" into a complete legal text, based on which both countries could draft implementing legislation. The deadline for the signature of the text was January 2 (since the U.S. authority for "fast track" congressional review of legislation submitted by the President to implement the agreement expired then at midnight under the U.S. Trade Act of 1974). Given the documents at issue, the negotiators faced a daunting task. The "Elements" was a 33-page paper that outlined the Agreement. The final text was a formal legal document of nearly 300 pages, with 21 chapters and numerous annexes. The atmosphere in which the negotiators worked was intense, and both governments were being pressed by constituents to reveal the details of FTA.

The task of drafting the Agreement was coordinated by the General Counsel's office of the U.S. Trade Representative (USTR) and Trade Negotiations Office (TNO). Each office assigned a team of lawyers to the task, and used work groups to handle specialized areas of the Agreement.

Drafts were written, exchanged, and reconciled in a tedious point-by-point, line-by-line process. Clearly, any such extensive drafting process revealed points on which governments had not reached a meeting of the minds. Negotiators therefore were reassembled at intervals during the autumn to hammer out additional understandings. The final such meeting at the political level took place in early December. Decisions were made on outstanding issues, which generally involved the dropping of difficult demands that each side had made of the other. The way was then clear for the Agreement. This concluded the negotiation.

In *fifth stage* the action shifted from diplomatic bargaining to domestic lawmaking. The FTA was signed by President Reagan and Prime Minister Mulroney on January 2, 1988, only hours before the U.S. fast track authority expired by law. It was then necessary to draft legislation in both countries to implement the Agreement.

Implementation was not expected to proceed easily in either country, especially in the United States. Under fast track procedures, Congress cannot offer amendments to the bill submitted by the President to implement a trade agreement. However, the Congress retains the right to reject the agreement by defeating the President's implementing bill. Furthermore, the Congress could hold the FTA hostage in bargaining over other trade matters (which is what many thought had occurred earlier when the Senate Finance Committee nearly killed the FTA negotiation before it had got started). Under the fast track procedures, Congress was required to vote on a fixed time schedule. However, the time was fixed in terms of *legislative* rather than *calendar* days, which often proceed slowly. Yet if the President too hastily submitted implementing legislation to start the clock running on the deadline for Congressional votes, without adequately consulting the Congress and ensuring adequate support, he risked its likely defeat. On the Canadian side, however, implementation was expected to be less problematic. The Mulroney Government had an absolute majority in the Commons, which in a parliamentary system would ensure it could pass legislation necessary to effect external agreements.

In the end, congressional implementation of the FTA in the United States went relatively smoothly. While the Administration encountered some substantial Congressional concerns and knotty legal problems, they were able to assuage the former and resolve the latter. On the other hand, the Agreement ran into wholly unpredictable problems in Canada. The Liberal Party, which held a majority in Canada's non-elected Senate, refused passage of the implementing legislation. This forced the Mulroney Government to fight an election on the issue. This incident was surprising, because by custom the Senate had not used its constitutional power to defeat major legislation. The balance of power in the Senate has subsequently changed, but the incident is a useful reminder that politics in democratic countries, no matter what the structure, have the potential to be unpredictable.

Issues of Process in the North American Free Trade Negotiations: the United States

Use of the Fast Track

In 1982, the United States sought to use a ministerial meeting of the General Agreement on Tariffs and Trade (GATT) as a vehicle to further open markets around the globe. The U.S. hoped to continue steps toward trade liberalization taken in the Tokyo Round of multilateral trade negotiations concluded in 1979.

However, the 1982 GATT Ministerial was widely considered a failure. The United States began to consider more bilateral and plurilateral initiatives that might supplement its multilateral approach to trade, embodied in the GATT.

The Trade Act of 1974, as amended, authorized the President to negotiate trade agreements, and provided for the consideration of any implementing bill under "fast track" procedures. Under the fast track, the President's bill could not be amended, and would be considered on an expedited timetable. As a result, the Congress would vote on the bill on an up-or-down, take-it-or-leave-it basis.

Following the failed GATT Ministerial in 1982, the U.S. and Israel negotiated a Free Trade Agreement, implemented in U.S. domestic law through such fast track legislation. With the Israeli agreement under its belt, the U.S. proceeded, at Canadian Prime Minister Brian Mulroney's request, to notify the Senate Finance and House Ways and Means Committees of its intention to enter into free trade negotiations with Canada. After a harrowingly close vote in the Finance Committee, the negotiations began slowly and then rushed toward a tentative conclusion on October 3, 1987, when the Elements of Agreement were agreed. As noted above, a full legal text was concluded by the end of that year, and President Reagan and Prime Minister Mulroney signed the USA-Canada Free Trade Agreement on January 2, 1988. It was implemented through a fast track bill enacted in 1988, and entered into force on January 1, 1989.

The fast track authority provided in the Trade Act of 1974 expired at midnight on January 2, 1988. It was renewed in the Omnibus Trade and Competitiveness Act of 1988, which authorized the President to enter into bilateral and multilateral trade negotiations aimed at achieving specified negotiating objectives. The 1988 Act provided fast track authority for any bill to implement agreements resulting from such negotiations, under certain conditions.

As under the Trade Act of 1974, a special condition for bilateral agreements continued to be that the President notify the Senate Finance and House Ways and Means Committees in advance of his intention to enter into negotiations. If either committee voted to disapprove such negotiations, implementing legislation would not be eligible for fast track consideration.

For both bilateral and multilateral agreements, fast track authority was provided until June 1, 1991 (provided the President notified the Congress of his intention to enter into an agreement by March 1, 1991, and indeed entered into an agreement by June 1). However, the 1988 Act further permitted the President to request an extension of the fast track by March 1, 1991. Provided neither the House of Representatives nor the Senate disapproved his request, fast track authority then would be available until June 1, 1993 (provided, again, the President notified the Congress of his intention to enter into an agreement by March 1, 1993, and entered into the agreement by June 1, 1993).

On March 1, 1991, the President requested the above described two-year extension of the fast track, principally for the North American free trade negotiations with Mexico and Canada and the delayed conclusion of the Uruguay Round multilateral trade negotiations. Although a fast track disapproval resolution was introduced in each body, the Senate rejected the resolutions by a vote of 36 to 59 on May 24. The House likewise rejected it, 192 to 231, on May 23. Consequently, President Bush enjoys fast track authority for two more years. He has until March 1, 1993, to notify the Congress of his intention to enter into an agreement with Mexico and Canada; and until June 1, 1993, to enter into an agreement. If he meets these conditions, the bill he submits to Congress to implement the agreement will be considered by the Congress under fast track procedures.

It is important to appreciate the strategy and direction of U.S. trade policy to understand initiatives toward bilateral and now trilateral free trade negotiations. While the multilateral GATT remains the cornerstone of the international trading system, the failure of the 1982 GATT Ministerial sparked more vigorous efforts by the United States to supplement the GATT with bilateral or plurilateral agreements. The current negotiations with Mexico and Canada are simply a next step in this trend, perhaps made more significant by the failure of GATT Contracting Parties to conclude the Uruguay Round multilateral trade negotiations at the Brussels Ministerial in December 1990 as scheduled.

The use of the fast track to implement trade agreements magnifies the role of the private sector in influencing their negotiation and implementation. The Administrations's need to obtain Congressional support, and its ability to avoid unravelling legislative amendments, explain much about the calculus it employs in formulating its strategy for trade negotiations and their legislative implementation.

The Private Sector

In the negotiation and implementation of a trade agreement with Mexico and Canada, the private sector enjoys two roles: a formal role, established in law; and a perhaps more significant informal role, ensured by the Administration's need to garner political support for the agreement and its implementing legislation.

The *formal* structure was devised in the Trade Act of 1974, to obtain private sector advice for the Administration throughout the Tokyo Round multilateral trade negotiations. The 1974 Act called for the establishment of Industry Sector Advisory Committees (ISACs). These ISACs were to include representatives of industry across a broad spectrum of economic activity, intended to ensure that the Administration would receive sound private sector advice.

The advisory committee system has been enhanced significantly over time. Currently, the structure includes an overall Advisory Committee on Trade Policy and Negotiations, as well as cross-sectoral or functional advisory committees on labour, agriculture, services, intellectual property protection, investment, defence and intergovernmental relations.

The Trade Act of 1974, as amended by the 1988 Omnibus Trade and Competitiveness Act, requires the President to seek the advice of these private sector groups in preparing for trade negotiations, developing negotiating positions, and evaluating any agreement achieved. Further, it provides for reports by these private sector groups to the Congress, to enable the Congress better to evaluate the agreements.

This system of private or public sector advisory committees thus provides a significant opportunity for the private sector to influence trade policy and negotiations. The breadth of the system ensures that advice is sought and received from a panoply of perspectives, and the regularity with which the system is used increases the likelihood that the input is timely and meaningful.

The membership of the various advisory committees is rotated regularly (normally every two years), and determined principally by the White House, including the Office of the U.S. Trade Representative; and the Department of Commerce. Persons interested in being considered for such positions may contact the Private Sector Liaison in the Office of the U.S. Trade Representative.

Also influential in the development of trade policy and conduct of trade negotiations are *informal* private sector groups, including specific companies, trade associations, or *ad hoc* coalitions of like-minded parties. The private sector gets effectively two bites at the apple of trade policy and negotiations, as a result of the Constitution's checks and balances of power. While the President enjoys the authority to conduct the foreign affairs of the United States, the Congress is authorized to regulate commerce with foreign nations. Since each branch has substantial power in shaping our trade policy and agreements, the private sector normally works closely with both bodies to maximize its input.

In addition to the two big bites at the executive and legislature, the organization of trade policy within the Executive Branch gives the private sector lots of little bites. Trade policy development is orchestrated, and negotiations led, by the Office of the U.S. Trade Representative in the Executive Office of the President. However, numerous agencies are involved, sometimes substantially, in negotiating trade agreements as well as implementing their provisions after entry into force.

The Bush Administration has continued the Economic Policy Council, chaired by the Secretary of the Treasury, as the principal Cabinet-level vehicle for resolving any disagreements among agencies about trade policy and negotiations. Just below the cabinet level, the inter-agency Trade Policy Review Group (TPRG), chaired by the Deputy U.S. Trade Representative, is the main engine for shaping the direction of trade policy and negotiations. Below the TPRG, the career Trade Policy Staff Committee conducts the day-to-day business of fashioning positions and texts of negotiating positions. These groups typically include, in addition to USTR, the Departments of State, Treasury, Commerce, Labor , Agriculture, Justice and Defense, Office of Management and Budget, and Council of Economic Advisers. Other agencies, such as Transportation and Energy, participate as appropriate.

Any private sector group seeking to influence negotiations thus has the opportunity to forum shop throughout the trade agencies of the Administration, to seek to enlist the most vigorous champion for its viewpoint and objectives. Simultaneously, the private sector may seek the support of members or committees of the Congress. Aware that it needs Congressional support for implementing legislation, the Administration takes careful account of the views of the Congress, particularly when expressed by committees of jurisdiction.

Private Sector Influence on the FTA

Examples of the private sector's influence in the negotiation and implementation of the USA-Canada Free Trade Agreement illustrate how the process worked before, and is likely to work again in the context of the negotiations with Mexico and Canada. Perhaps the broadest illustration of organized, cross-sectoral private sector support for the USA-Canada Agreement was an *ad hoc* coalition of companies called the ACTECAN--the American Coalition for Trade Expansion with Canada. Funded by major corporations (such as American Express Company) and enlisting the services of a consulting and media relations firm, the ACTECAN sponsored a symposium and rally for the Agreement at the U.S. Chamber of Commerce, encouraged expressions of support for the Agreement by companies to Members of Congress, explained the reasons for their support to major media editorial boards across the nation, and lobbied key members. ACTECAN activities helped to create the environment in which the USA-Canada Agreement was generally considered favourably.

In addition to ACTECAN activities, particular companies or industry associations expressed their support for the free trade negotiations, in the Administration and/or before the Congress. For example, written comments submitted in 1986 to the Subcommittee on Trade of the House Committee on Ways and Means included endorsements of the negotiations from, *e.g.*, Alcan Aluminum Corporation, Aluminum Company of America, American Furniture Manufacturers Association, American Paper Institute, American Telephone & Telegraph Company, Citizens for a Sound Economy, Deere & Company, Emergency Committee on American Trade, General Electric, GTE Corporation, Johnson Wax, Joseph E. Seagram & Sons, Motion Picture Association of America, National Association of Home Builders, National Association of Recycling Industries, National Marine Manufacturers Association, Outdoor Power Equipment Institute, Rice Millers' Association and Rockwell International.

In addition to such strong support for the negotiations, other U.S. private sector interests expressed to the Administration and/or the Congress at varying times their qualified or conditional support for the negotiations. Companies or groups in this category included, for example, the Committee on Pipe and Tube Imports, Cycle Parts and Accessories Association, National Cattlemen's Association, and PPG Industries (all of whom filed statements with the Subcommittee on Trade of the House Committee on Ways and Means). In each case, the company or industry group concerned identified its concerns regarding the free trade negotiations, and the conditions for its support for any agreement finally concluded.

A third category of U.S. private sector interests included those who concluded at an early date that their interests would not be benefitted by freer bilateral trade. Opposition was expressed in 1986 to the Subcommittee on Trade of the House Ways and Means Committee, for example, by the American Wire Producers Association, Coalition for Fair Lumber Imports, Committee to Preserve American Colour Television, International Leather Goods Plastics and Novelties Workers' Union, Lead-Zinc Producers Association, Luggage and Leather Goods Manufacturers of America, National Federation of Fishermen, Neckwear Association of America, and North Atlantic Fisheries Task Force.

Illustrative Private Sector Activity Throughout FTA Negotiations and Implementation

Autos

An example of private sector influence is presented by the automotive industry throughout the negotiation and implementation of the USA-Canada Agreement. From the outset, it was clear that a major issue would be how to deal with the USA-Canada Auto Pact, which had provided for duty-free trade in automobiles since 1965.

On the U.S. side, the Big Three, joined by the Motor Vehicle Manufacturers Association, Motor Equipment Manufacturers Association and United Auto Workers, played major roles. These groups met with both key officials in the Administration (especially at USTR and Commerce), as well as interested Members of Congress and their staffs--particularly members of the Michigan delegation, and especially Rep. John D. Dingell (D-Mi.), Chairman of the House Energy and Commerce Committee; Rep. Sander M. Levin (D-Mi.), a member of the House Ways and Means Committee; and Senator Carl M. Levin (D-Mi.).

Likewise automotive interests in Canada were particularly active in influencing the Canadian Government in its positions regarding the treatment of the Auto Pact. Of particular note from a U.S. perspective was the pressure on the Canadian Government from auto plants in Canada owned by third country interests. These "transplants" strongly opposed any increase in domestic content requirements to qualify for duty-free treatment beyond 50 percent. At the behest of the Canadian Government--indeed, with financial inducements from the Canadian Government--these companies had invested heavily in building and operating plants there, providing jobs for Canadians. They staunchly opposed losing their preferential access to the

U.S. market by requiring more U.S. and Canadian content than they were able to meet.

Equally fervid in their demand to raise the content requirement from 50 to 60 percent were U.S. automotive interests. So strong was their pressure, that negotiations were held at the eleventh hour in December in Ottawa, after the Elements of Agreement had been initialled on October 3, to try to persuade the Canadians to change their minds. Members of the Michigan delegation were consulted frequently throughout this exercise by USTR and Treasury negotiators in Ottawa. While Canadian-owned automotive interests were sympathetic, the opposition of the transplants in Canada prevailed, and the Canadian Government refused to raise the content level.

The U.S. interests did not give up, however, even after losing on this issue in the Agreement. They continued their campaign, principally through the Michigan Congressional delegation in Washington, and obtained several useful provisions in the implementing bill or accompanying Statement of Administrative Action ,[2] including explicit authority to negotiate with Canada to increase the automotive content requirement; special authority for the President to proclaim changes to the automotive content requirement; a study by USTR of Canadian automotive production-based duty remission programs; certain monitoring and reporting to the Congress; and the establishment of a "blue ribbon" private sector panel to make recommendations on the future of the North American automotive industry.

While the U.S. automotive interests seeking an increase in the content requirement to 60 percent have not yet achieved this goal, it was not for lack of sophisticated, tenacious and timely lobbying of both the Administration and the Congress.

Alcoholic Beverages

Another tough issue in the bilateral negotiations was alcoholic beverages. The USA was then the demander on this issue,[3] seeking liberalization by Canada of its restrictions on the internal sale and distribution of such

---

2　The Statement of Administrative Action is a document that the President must provide along with any implementing bill submitted to the Congress under fast track procedures. In it, the President is required to explain how a trade agreement will be implemented through administrative action, in addition to changes proposed in the implementing bill to U.S. legislation.

3　More recently, Canada has complained about allegedly GATT-legal practices of certain states and local governments in the United States.

beverages--effected principally by various provinces of Canada. On the Canadian side, the handling of this issue was complicated by the Canadian constitution's lack of provisions comparable to the U.S. Commerce Clause, making the U.S. Federal Government supreme over the states in regulating commerce among the states as well as with foreign nations.

The issue was further complicated in U.S. private sector politics by a sharp division among U.S. industry--those who had already established or licensed operations in Canada, vs. those who had not and were prevented from penetrating the Canadian market from the U.S. by Canadian provincial and federal restrictions. Perhaps in part because of this division, beer ultimately was not addressed in the Agreement, except to reaffirm each government's rights under the General Agreement on Tariffs and Trade with respect to beer trade.

Throughout the negotiations, U.S. private sector companies and groups interested in wine, beer and distilled spirits made known their views, most often at USTR, but at other agencies as well. Through such contacts, they were able to impress on the Administration their objectives in the negotiations, and maximize the advantages accruing to them through the Agreement.

Fish, Lobsters and Potatoes

Another example of private sector lobbying of the negotiations and their implementation is the efforts regarding fish, lobsters and potatoes (all fished or grown notably in Maine, home state of Senator George Mitchell, then an influential Member of the Finance Committee and now Senate Majority Leader). Even though freer trade serves the national economic interest, there can be particular companies or industries that consider themselves losers in a freer trade environment. Many Maine fishermen and potato farmers seemed to consider themselves in this category. They apparently felt they would be disadvantaged by increased imports from Canada of duty-free lobsters and potatoes.

As already noted, some of these private sector interests opposed the negotiations from their outset; for example, the National Federation of Fishermen and North Atlantic Fisheries Task Force opposed the negotiations if they were to include fisheries matters. Following the conclusion of the Agreement, these interests presumably were quite active in the "negotiation" between the Administration and Congress of the implementing legislation. In deliberations with the Senate Finance Committee, for example, Senator Mitchell proposed and the Finance Committee supported the inclusion of provisions: (a) authorizing the President to negotiate and implement reciprocal quantitative limits on the export and import of all potatoes in bilateral trade with Canada; and (b) prohibiting the entry into the U.S. customs territory of lobsters smaller than the minimum size under the American Lobster Fishery Management Plan. The Committee also supported a requirement for the President to take appropriate action with respect to Canadian export controls on unprocessed fish, to enforce U.S. rights under the GATT.

The House Ways and Means Committee did not include analogous provisions in its proposed implementing legislation. While it ultimately accepted the Senate Finance Committee provisions on potatoes and Canadian export controls on unprocessed fish, it declined to accept the measures regarding lobsters. In the document memorializing the resolution of differences between the committees, the proposed House/Senate Agreement reads simply: "No agreement reached." In light of the lack of agreement on lobster provisions between the two committees of jurisdiction, the Administration felt free not to include them in the bill the President ultimately submitted.[4] These measures, then, were not included in the implementing legislation.

Lumber

A longstanding source of bilateral friction was trade in lumber products. In 1983, the U.S. Commerce Department had found imports from Canada of certain softwood lumber products not to be subsidized. However, in a preliminary determination a few years later, Commerce tentatively concluded that such products were subsidized, and therefore subject to countervailing duties if such imports materially injured, or threatened material injury to, the U.S. industry producing such products. The latter proceeding under the U.S. countervailing duty law was short-circuited when the two governments entered into a memorandum of understanding (MOU) regarding lumber in 1986.

---

4   In correspondence between Secretary of the Treasury James A. Baker, III and U.S. Trade Representative Clayton Yeutter, on the one hand, and on the other hand the Speaker of the House of Representatives, Jim Wright; Majority Leader of the Senate, Robert Byrd; Chairman of the Committee on Ways and Means, Dan Rostenkowski; and Chairman of the Committee on Finance, Lloyd Bentsen, the Administration agreed "to accept the provisions worked out in the [fast track] consultative process [between the Administration and Congress], provided they are consistent with the Agreement and its implementation and are appropriate to carrying out its fundamental purposes." The lobster and potato provisions were not "worked out" in the consultative process between the Ways and Means and Finance Committees.

Many of the U.S. companies and associations interested in the lumber subsidy issue lobbied the Administration and Congress to support their objectives. For example, in 1986, prior to conclusion of the MOU, the Coalition for Fair Lumber Imports complained to the House Committee on Ways and Means of unfairly traded lumber imports from Canada, and urged the committee to withhold negotiating authority for the FTA (by voting to disapprove the negotiations). The Coalition opposed Canadian proposals to fold the lumber issue into the FTA talks, and urged Congress and the Administration to resolve the lumber issue before proceeding with FTA negotiations.

Following conclusion of the MOU in 1986 and FTA negotiations in 1987, the private sector lumber groups further lobbied the Congress and Administration concerning the implementing legislation. As a result, not surprisingly it includes provisions "grandfathering" the 1986 move and otherwise relating to lumber (although these provisions concern a bilateral dispute about plywood standards, rather than the subsidy issue).

Issues of Process in the North American Free Trade Negotiations: Canada

Private Sector

The Trade Act of 1974 structured the relations between the Federal Government and the constituents of trade policy in the United States. This structure worked well in the Tokyo Round negotiation, and it was substantially adopted by Canada in preparing for the bilateral free trade negotiation.

The Trade Act created an Advisory Committee on Trade Negotiations (ACTN) composed of leading business and labour leaders and designed to provide private-sector advice concerning trade negotiations. Below the ACTN were established a series of specialized committees to deal more intensively with specific sector concerns. Specialized committees dealt with agriculture, labour, and industry; and these areas were further broken down, such as in industry where some 27 Industry Sector Advisory Committees (ISACs) were formed. The structure operated hierarchically, and the ACTN was responsible for presenting the composite views of the private sector to Congress.

The advisory process created by the Trade Act of 1974 increased substantially the interaction between government and the private sector during trade negotiations, and it was well received on all sides. Business constituents supported it because it involved them more closely in trade policy, while Congress appreciated the fact that the numerous meetings between sector committees and trade officials deflected some constituency pressure from Congress to the executive. For its part, the executive branch trade bureaucracy found the advisory system increased work, but it made that work easier by bureaucratizing the constituency and making the task of dealing with conflicting pressures more transparent.

The advisory system facilitated U.S. passage of the Tokyo Round accords. In 1979 it was widely predicted that President Jimmy Carter would have trouble getting the Tokyo Round through Congress. However, the Trade Agreement Act of 1979 passed the House and the Senate by the lopsided votes of 395-7 and 90-4, respectively. An important reason for this widespread support is that the ACTN report to Congress on the Tokyo Round was entirely supportive of the negotiated agreements. Congress approved the agreements because the trade constituency -as represented by the ACTN report--felt they were consistent with U.S. interests.

The advisory system had several strong points. Even though it was intended to increase the influence of constituency groups over trade policy, it also facilitated the government's task of dealing with constituents. For one thing, the advisory system gave constituent groups a stake in the negotiation. Second, the system structured constituency relations for the government. One of the real problems for government is knowing exactly where pressures are going to come from. An additional problem is the ability to identify passive interests, that is, interests that you know are out there, but because they are not taking action in their own right you do not hear from them. The advisory system allowed government to get a more balanced picture of constituency demands. An example of this balancing was the liquor industry in the United States, which was generally divided during the Tokyo Round between domestic, largely whisky-producing companies that did not want liberalization and multinationals that supported liberalization. By bringing both groups together, the advisory system produced a different picture than if the government had heard only from the former group of the industry.

In January 1986, the Canadian Government established a private sector International Trade Advisory Committee (ITAC). Modelled after the ACTN in the United States, it included some 45 individuals representing large and small business, as well as various trade and consumer associations in Canada. Labour leaders, which were represented on the U.S. ACTN, generally refused to accept appointments to the Canadian ITAC, the sole exception being the president of the Canadian Federation of Labour.[5] The purpose of the ITAC was to broadly advise the Minister of International Trade on the conduct of trade policy and negotiations.

The following August the Canadian Government announced the creation of 15 Sector Advisory Groups on International Trade (SAGITs), again loosely modelled after the U.S. system. SAGITs were designed to provide sector-specific advice to government, and included the major industrial and service activities in the Canadian economy. Also included were representatives from agriculture, retailers and consumers. The 15 SAGITs and their membership are presented in table 2.

The Canadian ITAC/SAGIT system in the bilateral free trade negotiation functioned roughly the way the U.S. ACTN/SAC system had performed in the Tokyo Round; namely, it channelled and contained constituency pressures and helped the government to respond to specific demands from constituents in a more organized manner. More broadly, however, the main cleavage in the FTA negotiation was between those constituency groups that supported or opposed the Agreement itself, and the sector advisory system tended not to reflect the depth of the cleavage that eventually did develop. Most SAGITs supported the FTA, and for those that did not (such as textiles, cultural industries, and possibly consumer products) the electoral process provided a better mechanism for outright opposition than the advisory process.

It is unlikely that the constituency advisory system had as much impact on Canadian trade negotiation as it did on American negotiation. One reason is that--unlike the American side--the Canadian ITAC and SAGITs were not hierarchically integrated, which allowed government to deal directly with grass roots sector constituencies and reduced the capacity of the ITAC to aggregate sector interests and therefore to speak for the private sector as a whole. Even more important, however, there was no Canadian equivalent for the legislated power of the U.S. ACTN to provide Congress with an evaluation of trade agreements negotiated by the Executive, along with a recommendation for action. Since Congress would clearly be influenced by any such recommendation, this represented a substantial power for the ACTN in U.S. trade policy making. In Canada, the ITAC did not have the power to render a public advisory opinion as to whether or not the FTA served Canadian interests. To have given the ITAC such ACTN-like powers would have created problems internally for the Canadian Government, and

---

5   Subsequently, on June 21, 1989, five additional labour leaders accepted appointments on the ITAC.

Table 2 Membership of Canadian Sector Advisory Groups on International Trade (August, 1986)[a]

SAGITs	No. of SAGIT Members[b]	No. of Independent Business Reps.	Representatives of Boards, Associations &	No. of Union Reps.	Other Reps.
Total	248	173	44	11	20
Percent	100	69.8	17.7	4.4	8.1
Agriculture, Food & Beverage	37	10	26	0	1
Forest Products	18	16	2	0	0
Automotive & Aerospace Industries	17	13	2	0	2
Fish & Fish Products	16	8	6	2	0
Minerals & Metals	16	12	1	2	1
Energy Products & Services	16	13	0	1	2
Industrial, Marine & Rail Equipment	16	13	2	1	0

[a] Adapted from: Rugman, Alan M., and Andrew Anderson, "Business and Trade Policy: The Structure of Canada's New Private Sector Advisory System," *Canadian Journal of Administrative Sciences*, Vol. 4, No. 4, December 1987, p. 375; [b] excluding the chairperson.

Table 2 (continued)

SAGITs	No. of SAGIT Members[b]	No. of Independent Business Reps.	Representatives of Boards, Associations &	No. of Union Reps.	Other Reps.
Financial Services	16	15	0	0	1
Apparel & Fur	15	10	1	1	3
Communications, Computer Equipment & Services	15	15	0	1	0
General Services	14	10	1	1	2
Arts & Culture Industries	14	7	0	0	7
Chemicals & Petrochemicals	13	12	1	0	0
Textiles, Footwear & Leather	11	1	1	0	13
Consumer & Household Products	9	1	1	1	12

would have been viewed as inconsistent with the unitary control of Cabinet and the Federal bureaucracy over policy making. Because of the parliamentary system, the Canadian Government has greater control over trade policy than does the U.S. Administration. As a result, it was able to avoid giving the ITAC equivalent advisory powers that the ACTN enjoyed in the United States, with the result that constituency groups in Canada have less influence than U.S. groups have over trade policy.

Provincial Governments

Unlike state governments in the United States, provincial governments have become a major factor in Canada's external trade policy making. In the early stages of the Tokyo Round, provincial governments demanded greater access to the negotiation process and to the decisions that were being made. They were able to back this demand by a growth in provincial bureaucracies, particularly an increase in individuals expert in trade policy. It is through bureaucratic expertise that governments develop the capacity to analyze trade, and it is expertise, in turn, that increases the power of governments in a negotiating situation. The growth in provincial negotiating power occurred at the outset of the Tokyo Round when there were rumblings from Ontario that the sector approach to the tariff negotiation which the Federal Government was considering at the time was sharply against the interests of Ontario. There was a possibility that opposition from Ontario might have become public, which would have damaged the bargaining position of the Federal Government. It quickly became clear that there was a need to bring provincial bureaucrats, especially from Ontario, much more into the picture of the Tokyo Round negotiation.

In 1977, Canada established the Canadian Coordinator for Trade Negotiations (CCTN), which effectively operated as a secretariat for an ad hoc Cabinet committee created to supervise Canada's participation in the multilateral trade negotiation (MTN). The task of the CCTN was to liaise with constituency groups and provincial governments, and it did this job very well. During the Tokyo Round, many of the constituency pressures were directed not only to the Federal Government but also to provincial governments. Provincial governments became effectively a conduit for promoting constituency concerns within the province to the Federal Government. Thus the CCTN, which was initially set up to handle constituency relations, actually ended up dealing more with provincial bureaucracies, which in turn relayed demands from the private sector.

As Canada geared up for the FTA negotiations, it was clear the bilateral negotiations would touch more Canadian interests than previous multilateral negotiations had done. Therefore consultations with provincial governments was a political necessity for the Federal Government. This need was increased because of the development of knowledgeable trade bureaucracies in provincial governments. Prior to Canada's formal announcement of its intention to seek bilateral negotiations, meetings were held between Canada's first ministers to assess provincial concerns. These meetings revealed some substantive differences--e.g., Ontario and Manitoba were less enthusiastic about freer trade than the remaining provinces--but all provinces agreed on the procedural matter that provincial involvement in the negotiation should be maximized.

At the technical level, consultation between the Federal and provincial governments started well in advance of the negotiation with Washington. The Canadian negotiator--Simon Reisman--met with provincial representatives in January, 1985, and this forum was later regularized into what became known as the Continuing Committee on Trade Negotiations (CCTN). The provinces in turn appointed teams of bureaucrats to monitor their own concerns, and in some cases they named individuals with prominent trade backgrounds--such as Jake Warren in Quebec or Bob Lattimer in Ontario--to head up provincial teams.

The issue of provincial involvement came to a head in the First Ministers' conference in Halifax on June 2, 1987. Prior to the meeting, provincial governments had devised a plan for provincial participation which would have included participation at negotiation sessions, a veto over any matter that involved provincial jurisdiction, and participation in sessions that dealt with negotiating mandates or strategy. This plan was initiated by the Western provinces that had had a history of trade policy activism in the Tokyo Round, but it was a product of suspicions shared by other provinces as well. Quebec supported provincial involvement by instinct; Ontario, which was not enthusiastic about a free trade negotiation, sought provincial involvement to monitor the Federal Government; and the Western provinces, which supported free trade, wanted provincial involvement to monitor Ontario and to prevent any collusion it might attempt with the Federal Government. The Federal Government firmly resisted these demands and instead laid out a position that provided maximum consultation and exchange of information, but no seat at the negotiating table nor involvement in establishing mandates or strategies for negotiators. It became clear at the Halifax First Ministers' Meeting that for the provinces to continue to push for provincial involvement would risk compromising the negotiation, and therefore Quebec (where free trade was enthusiastically supported by the business community) and the Western provinces reluctantly agreed to climb down from their extreme position. This isolated Ontario, and in the end the Federal position carried the day, but it created an obligation for the Federal Government to make good on the promise of full provincial participation.

It was never clear what "full provincial participation" meant, but the Federal Government chose to deal fulsomely with the process of consultation in the hopes that the other more troublesome aspects of participation would resolve themselves. A senior officer was appointed to the Trade Negotiation Office (TNO) exclusively with the task to conduct liaison with provincial governments. Meetings were initiated by provinces on various issues of substance, and were held bilaterally with the Federal Government or multilaterally as needed. The TNO initiated formal meetings of the CCTN before all of the 17 negotiating sessions with the United States negotiators, and then followed up each negotiating session with a conference call to all ten provincial representatives. These conference calls were known to have been taped and transcribed by the Ontario government, and these transcripts were generally regarded as the best record of the negotiation produced in Canada.

Full consultation did not end provincial demands for participation and the tensions between Federal and provincial governments continued into the negotiation. On substantive issues like automotive trade or energy, provincial governments felt they represented the constituency better than the Federal Government. On issues of adjustment, provincial governments (especially Ontario) were distressed at the Federal disinclination to deal with the perceived downside of freer trade. Provincial concerns led to demands that provincial bureaucrats be assigned office space in the TNO headquarters, with full rights to attend internal briefings, and informal negotiating sessions with U.S. negotiators. The TNO continued to flatly oppose these demands.

On the other side of the coin, provincial representatives had to recognize their involvement was much greater than what had occurred in the past. In addition to verbal consultations, there was a major exchange of documents during the FTA, which included some 700 documents transmitted from the Federal Government to the provinces. Even some documents headed for Cabinet were passed on to the provinces, with the headings changed appropriately not to compromise the formalities of Cabinet secrecy. This exchange convinced most provincial participants that Federal-provincial liaison had changed dramatically from an earlier period of Canadian trade negotiation, when, as a former Federal civil servant noted about the Kennedy Round, "the provinces got told when everyone else got told." The fact is, had the Federal Government continued with Kennedy

Round-type practices, it would not have had the political legitimacy to conclude the FTA.

In the end, most of the FTA negotiation fell within the legal jurisdiction of the Federal Government. The power experienced by provincial governments was largely political and not legal, although the prospect that some issues that involved provincial jurisdiction might be raised justified their political concern. The only major issue that touched on provincial jurisdiction was Chapter 8 of the FTA that dealt with wine and distilled beverages, and it especially affected Ontario, the province most opposed to the negotiation. Ontario threatened a court challenge over Chapter 8 which, had it been successful, could have seriously compromised the capacity of Canada to participate in trade negotiations in the future. In the event, the case was not brought, and the reason is that it was probably too risky for the provinces and for Ontario. There was considerable legal support for the argument that the constitutional power to deal with trade lay with the Federal Government, which gave that government the right to negotiate and implement trade agreements. Had Ontario lost the case, it would have undercut legal justification for provincial participation in future trade negotiations, and all for alcoholic beverages which is not a central trade concern of the provinces. On the other hand, if Ontario had won the case it could have been a Pyrrhic victory, since it would have chilled the cooperation and exchange of information that had developed in the FTA, and which went arguably well beyond the legal obligation of the Federal Government. The alcoholic beverages issue reflected the limits to which provincial participation was carried in the FTA, but the fact that the issue nearly went to the courts demonstrates the constraints on contemporary Canadian trade negotiation.

Public opinion

Once the FTA was signed, it had to be approved in both countries. On the U.S. side this is always a problem because Congress, which does not negotiate trade agreements, nevertheless has the Constitutional power to regulate commerce with foreign nations and pass legislation. In Canada, with a parliamentary system, one would expect a government with a solid majority to be able to ratify any agreement it negotiated. This did not occur because the opposition Liberal party chose to use its then majority in Canada's unelected Senate to thwart the Parliament, and to force an election over the FTA. The election constituted an exceptionally stern democratic test of the FTA. In effect it was a laboratory from which lessons can be learned regarding the public's reaction to trade agreements.

The state of public opinion was critical to the eventual success of the FTA. Before the negotiation was announced, free trade was a solid choice among Canadian respondents in Gallup polls. In polls that had produced roughly similar results since the mid-1950s, slightly over half of Canadians felt they would be better off with free trade, around 30 per cent felt they would be worse off, and the remainder was made up of undecideds. Just before the Progressive Conservative victory in 1984, polls were recording support up to three-quarters in favour of free trade with the United States. However, once the negotiation was underway, support for free trade slipped, and attitudes pro and con were nearly equal when the election of 1988 was called. Concern was expressed in the more recent polls over the impact of free trade on Canada's sovereignty, and over the ability of the Progressive Conservative government to negotiate a good deal with the United States.

One reason for the decreasing dominance of the pro free trade position is that the undecided respondents, which over two decades had been around 20 percent, apparently went mainly to the anti-free trade side. This may have occurred because the negotiation created much media attention for free trade, which in turn brought forth a lot of negative commentary about a policy concept that had previously been treated with indifference by politicians and press alike. A more probable reason, however, is that the free trade process inevitably involved a negotiation, and negotiations--as recently demonstrated by the Meech Lake process in Canada--are not a popular form of policy making in a democracy. Negotiations necessarily require that decisions be made by a small group, and secrecy is inherent to the process. Negotiations create excitement which tends to attract the press, but since little hard information can be given to the press the resulting news reports are not as informative as the press or their readership would prefer. In this atmosphere it is easy for a climate of suspicion to develop, which creates a supportive environment for those opposed to the negotiation. Governments have great difficulty in dealing with this climate of suspicion, because they cannot explain the details of a negotiation without compromising the process.

Once the FTA was signed it was immediately made public. The TNO had prepared a public relations strategy for the release of the FTA which included many appearances by the Chief negotiator Simon Reisman. However the government was unprepared for the magnitude of criticism and hostile debate that the FTA triggered. The negative backlash caused the government to lose control of the agenda, and to create an impression in the public that the Prime Minister assumed the FTA would stand on its own without public explanation or debate. In retrospect, it appears the government's strategy for the public launch was inadequate. The situation the FTA faced in Canada was an opposition that had been frustrated throughout the negotiation by a lack of information, and which was then primed to respond once the document was released with an intensity normally reserved for democratic electoral contests. The media responded to this opposition largely because it was a legitimate source of news. Against this opposition the government initially sought to explain the FTA, and it mainly used as a spokesman the chief negotiator who necessarily would be more attuned to the details of the Agreement than to the context of public opinion into which the Agreement was being placed. The impression created was that of a contest between the government that used the tactics of explanation and an opposition that used the tactics of electioneering.

The FTA generated a major organizational response among those opposed to it. In 1985 the anti-free trade interests coalesced into a group known as the Council of Canadians (COC), which grew out of an earlier, pro-nationalist group known as the Committee for an Independent Canada (CIC). The COC was open to individual membership, but as an indication of the strength of the anti-free trade movement, the COC in 1987 merged into the Pro-Canada Network (PCN), an umbrella organization composed of social groups drawn largely from the women's movement, environmentalists, labour, and the churches. With the hierarchy of groups that it represented, the PCN had no difficulty in generating visibility for the opposition to free trade. The PCN tactics were to seek media debates, and to support candidates of the opposition parties that came out prominently against free trade. The most effective action taken by the PCN was to publish a cartoon-style booklet in the style of a comic book that alternately lampooned and savaged the notion of a trade agreement between Canada and the United States. The booklet made effective use of humour and it played heavily on the theme of the loss of Canadian sovereignty and Canadian values to the vastly larger U.S. presence. For many people who did not understand the FTA, the PCN comic book represented the most clearly-presented argument on free trade they had seen. To say that it was an effective device in shaping mass opinion would be an understatement.

Proponents of the FTA were deeply distressed over the distortions in the public debate over the FTA. On the one hand, issues of social policy were brought into the debate that had never before been associated with trade policy, while on the other hand the public seemed ignorant of the limitations on Canadian decision making automony that Canada had already accepted by joining the GATT and the International Energy Agreement. The distortions were so extreme in the public debate that many FTA proponents felt the media was biased and was deliberately contributing to the negative side. This accusation was probably wrong, for studies on the media have shown that even though there were some organs (such as the Toronto *Star*) that took a one-sided approach, most newspaper and TV coverage was essentially balanced and reported both sides of the debate. What appeared as bias was simply the reportage of the range and intensity of the debate, which went well beyond anything that could have been predicted.

The public debate over the FTA was not so much over free trade as it was a debate over alternative fundamental policies for the nation. The way to appreciate this point is to ask why were women's groups and environmentalists, which normally have never been associated one way or another with trade concerns, so opposed to the FTA? The reason is that the FTA raised the symbolic question of promoting the free market at the expense of government interventionism in the economy, whereas women's groups and environmentalists see their concerns as being threatened by the private market and advanced only through an interventionist government. It is understandable that the FTA might have triggered this more fundamental debate, since from the Macdonald Commission onward, free trade had been viewed explicitly as a move in the direction of more market-oriented policies.

The major themes in the attack on the FTA were loss of sovereignty and the threat to social programs, and both themes are obviously related to the role of government in the economy. Of the two, the alleged threat of free trade to social programs like medicare or child-care services were the most effective argument of the anti-FTA lobby. Although the government tried to neutralize these threats--for example, by soliciting the testimony of former Chief Justice Emmett Hall that the FTA posed no threat to medicare- it was nevertheless difficult to counter an argument based on fear with one based on reasoned analysis. In the end, the government itself used an argument based on fear--namely, the fear of economic isolation and stagnation--which appeared to have more impact with ordinary Canadians than more sophisticated economic arguments had done.

Lessons From the FTA Experience: Extension to Mexico

Private Sector

What is past is often prologue. The negotiation and fast track implementation of the USA-Canada Free Trade Agreement foreshadow a great deal of the substance and procedures likely to be employed in connection with the negotiations with Mexico and Canada. U.S. companies and industries interested in these talks as a vehicle for their objectives, then, may be well advised to profit from the private sector lobbying experience in connection with the USA-Canada Free Trade Agreement.

Companies or groups in the United States seeking to influence the free trade negotiations with Mexico and Canada should formulate their objectives and generate support for them in the Administration and Congressional committees of jurisdiction. When appropriate, they may also consider coordinating with their counterparts in Mexico and Canada so as to influence the negotiations from the other sides of the border as well. Congressmen can be urged to write letters to the Administration; one agency can be urged to write another; studies can be conducted or requested; speeches can be delivered from the floor of the House or Senate, directed to the Administration or the Governments of Mexico and Canada. The higher priority an issue is for a company or group, the more paths it may pursue to achieve it.

Once the talks are concluded, the Congressional-Administration "negotiation" of an implementing bill affords other, possibly broader, opportunities, for U.S. private sector interests. A company with a legislative agenda--whether or not directly related to issues on the USA-Mexico-Canada FTA negotiating table--may find the fast track an attractive vehicle for enactment of its agenda. In 1988, the Administration ultimately accepted provisions in the legislation to implement the Canada Agreement that were unnecessary (and in some cases, unappreciated by the Government of Canada). To ensure passage of the implementing bill by both the House and Senate, the Administration might be willing to add a provision here or there that it would otherwise be reluctant to support.

The time is ripe, then, for U.S. companies and trade associations to consider how the free trade negotiations with Mexico and Canada may be useful to accomplish their objectives. They would be well advised to consider as well how to try to preclude other interests from using those negotiations in ways that may be harmful to their objectives.

Public Sector

The main concern regarding a North American Free Trade Agreement is that the negotiation process will be more politicized, especially in the United States, than was the Canada-USA FTA. In Canada, it is unlikely a negotiation with Mexico will heighten the amount of public anxiety that was aroused in the previous bilateral negotiation, but already it is clear that opposition to a trilateral agreement is building toward a major confrontation. In both countries, and especially in the United States, it will be necessary for governments to develop a sound strategy for generating support for the negotiation internally while the external negotiation is being conducted.

Canada and the United States will undoubtedly make use of their respective advisory systems to maintain contact with the private sector. Due to the differing impact of constituency pressures on trade policy, this will be more important in the United States than Canada. The Canada-USA FTA attracted substantial pressure from constituency groups on transportation services, automotive products and cultural services, but for the most part the FTA was not subject to the intense lobbying that is often associated with U.S. trade policy. This is less likely to be the case with a trilateral negotiation, and areas that already look difficult (in addition to the above three) include agriculture, business travel, energy and dispute settlement. In order to negotiate effectively, the United States will have to maximize the opportunities for consultation provided in the constituency advisory system. On the Canadian side, a mechanism for dealing politically with provincial governments similar to that conducted by the TNO will have to be put in place for the trilateral negotiation.

A major difficulty that will be presented in a trilateral negotiation is the need to develop a PR plan to develop public support for an agreement. The reason such a plan is necessary is that public opinion can bring independent pressures on Congressional decisions on trade policy beyond those pressures that might be faced from economic constituents directly concerned with the policy. In past negotiations such as the FTA or even the Tokyo Round, the general public was not an important player in trade policy. However, in the recent effort to secure fast track for the trilateral negotiation, the Administration was forced to respond to general public concerns about environment, immigration and economic adjustment in order to gain Congressional support for the negotiations. These issues will now have to be dealt with during the negotiation, and other issues may be forced onto the agenda before the negotiation is concluded.

It will be necessary for governments to improve their ability to deal with the political and PR aspects of the North American Free Trade negotiation. The Canadian experience in the FTA suggests that if governments wait until an agreement is reached to deal with public criticism of the negotiation, it may be too late to recover public confidence in the negotiation. Governments should increase their capacity to understand the context of public opinion in which trade agreements will be debated (such as, for example, the perceived threat of freer trade to social programs in Canada); and then to develop a PR strategy to counter the more extreme and implausible criticisms of trade agreements.

Summary

Those who fail to learn from history are doomed to repeat it. As the North American Free Trade negotiations begin, public and private interests alike should benefit from the bilateral FTA learning curve and the following lessons.

First, do not underestimate the impact of seemingly irrelevant issues. Following the fast track extension debate on environmental and labour issues, it is clear that the North American Free Trade talks will be expected (albeit unreasonably) to resolve any and all issues of concern, not just trade issues. Illicit drug trafficking, debt burdens, any privatization problems, drought or flooding along the border, immigration issues, health and safety standards--you name it, and someone will ask why this or that problem was not resolved in the Free Trade Agreement.

Second (and a corollary of lesson number one), do not underestimate the battle of expectations. No matter how much trade negotiators accomplish, the gist of a mutually satisfactory trade agreement among sovereign governments with sometimes conflicting objectives is, inescapably, compromise. That means that no one government can meet all its goals, and some interests will be disappointed by the shortfall. Trade negotiators need to keep the focus on how far they have travelled, not how far they still have to go; on what any agreement achieves, rather than the remaining problems it fails to resolve.

Third, devise a plan for handling the PR aspect of the negotiation. In addition to consulting with primary constituents, trade officials now have to deal with generalized pressure groups (such as environmentalists) that adopt trade issues as one of their public concerns. This means trade officials must be able to anticipate the lines along which criticism will form, and be able to meet that criticism with effective public communications and salesmanship. One important PR strategy may be to decouple free trade from a general attack on government interventionism in the economy. The task should be to isolate protectionists, and to break up the coalition such as formed in Canada during the FTA negotiation between protectionists (who support government intervention in the economy) and environmental or other social groups (who also support government intervention, but for different reasons).

Fourth, consult, consult, consult with the Congress in the United States and with provincial governments in Canada. Such consultations are judged by the party consulted with rather than the consulting Executive Branch agency. For example, before, during and following the Canada-USA negotiations, and throughout the legislative implementation exercise, the

U.S. Administration felt it had set new records and scaled new heights in regularly, meaningfully consulting with the Congress. Yet the widespread charge on Capitol Hill was that the consultations were too few and superficial. The U.S. Administration needs to determine how much energy and resources it can and should devote to Congressional consultations--and then triple or quadruple this commitment.

Fifth, keep your eyes on both the forest and the trees. While each government needs a vision, or overview, of what it seeks to accomplish in a North American FTA, it also needs to identify the individual issues of key political and economic concern in the legislature and private sector, and to address them satisfactorily. From the outset, each government should anticipate the major concerns about what is likely to be included in a North American FTA, and then determine what it can do--within the agreement, its implementation or otherwise--to ameliorate, if not eliminate, those concerns.

Sixth, in the United States, give the U.S. Congress--particularly key committee chairs and ranking Republican members--as large a role as possible in ultimately drafting the implementing bill and other documents required. Under the U.S. Constitution, the Congress, with its power to regulate commerce with foreign nations, is a partner of the President, with his power to conduct the foreign affairs. If the Executive Branch treats the Congress like a partner, the Congress is more likely to appreciate its stake in both the partnership and its fruits, a North American Free Trade Agreement. Partners are far more likely to support rather than oppose their joint work product.

Seventh, stay creative!   But for the eleventh hour proposal for binational review of national antidumping and countervailing duty determinations, the Canada-USA Free Trade Agreement would have perished in the fall of 1987. The overriding lesson of the U.S.-Canada FTA negotiations is: where there is a will, there is *always* a way. And where there is so much at stake, surely the will exists.

Chapter 3

NAFTA: Questions of Form and Substance

Jeffrey J. Schott and Gary Clyde Hufbauer[1]

Introduction

On 11 June 1990, Presidents George Bush and Carlos Salinas de Gortari agreed to pursue the negotiation of a free trade agreement (FTA). Exactly one year later talks began--and a third country, Canada, also took a seat at the negotiating table. Even before the talks started, the process of crafting a North American Free Trade Agreement (NAFTA) accelerated from the incremental approach of melding separate bilateral FTAs between individual countries into a full-fledged trilateral negotiation.

While there are many historical examples of successful and unsuccessful attempts at bilateral and regional free trade agreements, there is little precedent for a trilateral arrangement.[2] In part the explanation is simple:

---

1   This paper is a slightly abridged version of chapter two of the forthcoming study, *North American Free Trade: Issues and Recommendations*, by Gary Clyde Hufbauer and Jeffrey J. Schott, to be published by the Institute for International Economics in December 1991.

2   There have been only two examples in the postwar period: the Benelux Economic Union between Belgium, Luxembourg, and the Netherlands (which has been overshadowed by their participation in the European Community); and the ill-fated East African Community (EAC) between Kenya, Tanzania, and Uganda. The EAC was established in 1967, but broke down despite the common colonial heritage of its partner countries and effectively came to an end in 1977.

it is easier to reach agreement among two countries than three; and it is easier to conclude a regional accord because more countries offer concessions in return for preferences received.[3]

A trilateral negotiation is inherently more unwieldy than the alternatives. But certain advantages compensate for the added complexity of initiating trilateral rather than bilateral negotiations. The accord can cover more issues (if at least two countries have an interest); compromises can be crafted among three countries in areas where the rift between two countries is too wide; and the negotiating outcome can reflect a variety of permutations and combinations.

Moreover, a trilateral negotiation is not wedded to a single document as the final outcome. Instead, the provisions can be applied on a selective basis; and the obligations can be phased in according to differential timetables.

Negotiators of a North American Free Trade Agreement (NAFTA) start off with a blank page. Given access to new computer technologies, they can quickly transform that page (or screen!) into a variety of forms. This chapter examines some of the options available to the U.S., Canadian, and Mexican negotiators, and the critical issues that will influence the shape of the final negotiating package. It also addresses the issue of extending FTA preferences to other countries in the future, either through accession to the NAFTA or through supplemental negotiations by one or more of the NAFTA signatories.

The Road to NAFTA

If one were to follow historical precedents, the road to NAFTA would likely proceed first to a USA-Mexico FTA before wending its way to a trilateral pact. Throughout the 1980s, Mexico seemed to follow the Canadian model of pursuing closer economic integration with the United States in incremental steps. As Canada moved from sectoral talks to FTA negotiations, Mexico too entered into a series of negotiations with the United States--moving from the specific (e.g., subsidies and countervailing duties in 1985), to sectoral talks under bilateral framework agreements in 1987 and 1989, then to the pursuit of an FTA in 1990.

---

3 Whereas it is rare to find three countries with approximately balanced mutual trade interests, each country may have a more-or-less balanced relationship with the region as a whole.

At the same time, Canada and Mexico began to pursue closer bilateral trade relations. In March 1990, Canadian and Mexican officials negotiated a series of framework accords that paralleled arrangements worked out between Mexico and the United States. Even then, however, Canadian Prime Minister Brian Mulroney did not anticipate trilateral negotiations in the near term: "Whether this emerges into a more formalized association with North America *over the next decade* [emphasis added], I don't know... But I wouldn't be scandalized at the prospect."[4]

The announcement on 11 June 1990 that the United States and Mexico intended to negotiate a bilateral FTA, and the subsequent launching on 27 June 1990 of the Enterprise for the Americas Initiative (EAI), raised the prospect of a series of new FTAs between the United States and other countries in the Western Hemisphere. These initiatives confronted Canada with the choice of either joining the "hub" (i.e., engaging trilateral negotiations) or becoming just a "spoke" in the U.S. FTA system.[5] In early 1991 Canada opted for the negotiation of a regional trade pact; and on 5 February 1991 President Bush announced that the three countries would initiate negotiations on a NAFTA.[6] Trilateral negotiations commenced in Toronto on 12 June 1991.

Substantive Determinants of NAFTA

In principle, the NAFTA negotiators start off *tabula rasa*, but in fact the model of the Canada-USA FTA will substantially influence the new agreement. Nineteen negotiating groups under six broad categories have been established (see Annex A). The type of agreements reached, however, will depend both on the extent to which the existing Canada-USA FTA is augmented and on efforts to unravel present FTA obligations. For example,

---

4   As quoted by Canadian Press, 19 March 1990.

5   Ronald J. Wonnacott ("U.S. Hub-and-Spoke Bilaterals and the Multilateral Trading System," *Commentary*, Toronto: C.D. Howe Institute, October 1990) puts forward an elegant discussion of the implications for Canada of a series of bilateral FTAs between the United States and third countries. In brief, he argues that most of the benefits accrue to the "hub" country (the United States) that negotiates FTAs with a number of countries; by contrast, the "spoke" countries continue to face barriers in each other's market while their trade preferences in the U.S. market are undercut by increased competition from other "spokes."

6   *Wall Street Journal*, 6 February 1991, p. A8.

if one of the negotiating partners objects to proposed additions or deletions to the agenda, the negotiating process may proceed bilaterally in that area.

Augmenting the FTA Model

Both the United States and Canada agree that their FTA can be improved upon, although they differ as to where and how.[7] The NAFTA is likely to augment the FTA model in at least three specific areas: intellectual property (IP), environmental issues, and subsidy/countervail and antidumping issues.[8]

Intellectual Property

The Canada-USA FTA contains only two specific provisions relating to intellectual property (IP) issues: one resolves a bilateral dispute relating to copyrights on the retransmission of broadcasts; the other sets out a hortatory commitment by both countries to pursue a strong IP agreement in the Uruguay Round. A more extensive chapter setting out IP rights and obligations was dropped from the agreement late in the negotiations, in large part due to U.S. concerns about Canadian requirements for the compulsory licensing of pharmaceutical patents under law C-22. This area has also been a problem in U.S.-Mexican relations, but was substantially resolved by the passage of new Mexican patent, trademark, and copyright laws in June-July 1991.

Given the prominence accorded IP issues in the Uruguay Round talks, and the formation of a separate IP negotiating group for the trilateral negotiations, an IP chapter will almost certainly be included in the NAFTA. At a minimum, the IP chapter will likely obligate the parties to accede to the prospective Uruguay Round agreement on intellectual property, or to accept obligations comparable to those currently under negotiation in the GATT.

The United States will seek to incorporate detailed obligations in NAFTA that "lock in" the recent Mexican IP reforms and that establish a

---

7   Indeed, the FTA *already* has been augmented twice by agreements to accelerate the implementation of tariff cuts on hundreds of products.

8   In the first session of the NAFTA talks in Toronto on 12 June 1991, the three countries agreed that intellectual property would be one of six broad areas under negotiation, and that subsidy issues would be dealt with under the rubric of trade rules. See *Journal of Commerce*, 13 June 1991, p. 1A.

model for both bilateral and regional accords in the Western Hemisphere (and in the GATT if the Uruguay Round is still in train). In addition, it will likely again press Canada to modify its compulsory licensing practices. By contrast, Canada may well try to limit the NAFTA to general commitments and defer specific obligations to the multilateral negotiations. At the end of the day, however, Canada will likely limit compulsory licensing to extreme situations, and thus remove the main obstacle to a NAFTA accord in this area.

Environment

The "Action Plan" submitted by President Bush to the Congress on 1 May 1991, during the U.S. debate on fast track authority, commits the United States to deal with a broad range of environmental concerns both in trade talks with Mexico and in "parallel" negotiations. The Canada-USA FTA provides no precedent in this area, although both countries dealt with the acid rain problem in a separate bilateral forum.[9] Among the negotiating groups organized to start the NAFTA process, environmental issues are likely to arise primarily in the groups dealing with "trade rules," health and safety standards, and agriculture.

While many of the environmental problems cited during the fast track debate are inherently bilateral, the NAFTA could set forth common provisions to guide national responses to trade-related environmental issues (involving, for example, minimum health and safety standards for products entering international commerce), and procedures for increasing the rigour of those standards throughout the region. The environmental area seems amenable to the Canada-USA FTA approach set out for financial services, in which both partner countries agreed on common principles supplemented by separate commitments by each to specific reforms of national policies and practices.

Subsidy/Countervail and Antidumping

The FTA committed Canada and the United States to negotiate new substantive rules in these areas over a five to seven year period; however,

---

9   Title IV of the U.S. Clean Air Act Amendments of 1990, signed into law on 15 November 1990, provides strict new guidelines for sulphur dioxide and nitrous oxide emissions and requires significant cuts in those emissions from 1980 levels. The United States and Canada subsequently entered into a framework agreement in March 1991 that dealt with acid rain and other air quality issues.

those talks have been effectively frozen pending the outcome of the Uruguay Round (where negotiators are likely to achieve, at best, only minor revisions to the Tokyo Round codes). In the interim, the dispute settlement provisions of FTA Chapter 19 have been used to deal with bilateral problems regarding the implementation of existing national laws and regulations.[10]

The prospect of meagre results in Geneva puts the ball squarely back in the NAFTA court. Progress toward closer regional integration in North America will again focus attention on several key subsidy issues, especially regional aids (including subfederal subsidies), adjustment assistance programs, and investment incentives.[11] Given the shared interest of Mexico and Canada in greater discipline on the use by the United States of countervailing duties, both may be amenable to subsidy reforms that go beyond what is achievable in the GATT round.[12] In particular, they may be willing to accept some limitations on purely domestic subsidies in exchange for a different U.S. approach to the issues of causation and injury, and perhaps the incorporation of a *de minimis* test by which cases are terminated if the calculated subsidy effect is below a certain threshold (say 2.5 percent).

In the antidumping area, however, the same obstacles that block progress in the GATT are likely to surface in the NAFTA negotiations. U.S. industries remain wary about predatory pricing practices of competing firms based in Mexico and Canada. With industrial lobbyists in mind,

10   Dispute settlement is discussed later in this chapter. For a more detailed discussion of the FTA provisions, see the introductory chapter by Jeffrey J. Schott, and the chapter by Gary Horlick, Geoffrey Oliver, and Debra Steger on dispute resolution mechanisms, in Jeffrey J. Schott, and Murray G. Smith, eds., *The Canada-United States Free Trade Agreement: The Global Impact*, Washington and Halifax: Institute for International Economics, Institute for Research on Public Policy, 1988.

11   In addition, the Canadian decision to abrogate the 1986 agreement with the United States on softwood lumber will resuscitate the contentious dispute over stumpage subsidies. See *Journal of Commerce*, 4 September 1991, p. 1A.

12   During the period 1980-1989, the United States initiated 15 CVD cases against Canadian products and 26 against Mexican products. However, no new cases have been brought against Mexican products since the 1985 bilateral agreement on subsidies and CVDs. See Weintraub, Sidney, *A Marriage of Convenience: Relations between Mexico and the United States*, New York, NY: Twentieth Century Fund, 1990, pp. 81-82; and US International Trade Commission (USITC), *Review of Trade and Investment Liberalization Measures by Mexico and Prospects for Future United States-Mexican Relations*, Publication 2275, Washington, DC: April 1990, pp. 4-19.

Congress is loath to consider reforms of U.S. antidumping laws, even when limited to FTA partners. Given the limited number of U.S. cases applied against Mexican and Canadian firms in recent years, and the relatively light Canadian and Mexican caseload,[13] one may question whether reform of antidumping practices is worth the political fight.[14]

While one may argue that in an FTA it would be better to introduce common competition policies to regulate predatory practices in intraregional trade rather than apply antidumping duties, such an approach seems beyond the pale of the present talks. Rather, the elimination of antidumping actions on intraregional trade (the approach adopted in the European Community) should be made a long term goal of the NAFTA, and considered in future trilateral (and multilateral) negotiations once the NAFTA is up and running. A companion long-term goal is to seek a closer approximation of competition policies among the NAFTA partners.

In the first stage, however, the NAFTA accord should work to extend the special dispute resolution rules and panel procedures of the Canada-USA FTA to Mexico (see discussion below). As in the intellectual property area, NAFTA provisions may also supplement the GATT obligations of the three countries, and thus provide a building block for future multilateral negotiations.

Unravelling the FTA Model?

The risk that NAFTA talks will unravel existing FTA provisions is most prominent in the energy sector and with regard to cultural industries; in both instances, exceptions from the FTA investment provisions could become targets for review.[15] In addition, the complex web of origin rules

13 Since 1985, the United States has initiated 17 and eight antidumping cases against Canadian and Mexican producers respectively; Canada has brought 25 cases against the United States; and Mexico has initiated 15 cases against U.S. firms.

14 Because antidumping cases affect only a fraction of a percent of bilateral trade in North America, Michael Stein (former general counsel of the USITC) has compared FTA attempts to proscribe antidumping cases to "trying to find a cure for which there is no known disease." See *International Trade Reporter*, 20 March 1991, p. 441.

15 At the initial NAFTA negotiating session, U.S. Trade Representative Carla Hills stated that "the only thing that's off the table is the ownership of the mineral rights in Mexico and US immigration laws." Both Canada and Mexico contested the U.S. position, adding to the list Canadian cultural industries and exploitation of Mexican energy resources, respectively. See *Journal of Commerce*, 13 June 1991, p. 1A; 18 June 1991, p. 3A.

spelled out in FTA Chapter 3 and its annexes will need to be revisited; pressures are already building to significantly increase local content requirements.[16]

Rules of Origin

Trilateral rules are essential for a NAFTA to work. To be sure, as the gap between most-favoured-nation (MFN) tariffs and the zero tariff for FTA partners is reduced, origin rules become less important. However, even in a world of zero MFN tariffs, rules of origin remain important to avert circumvention of trade remedy laws (a key issue in some antidumping and countervailing duty cases). In the meantime, origin rules are particularly important in sectors where MFN protection remains high.[17]

Divergent national interests and sectoral protectionist pressures make this issue potentially contentious. The problem will be to balance competing goals: encouraging foreign investment in the region while preventing third countries from using Mexico as a pure "export platform" to the United States and Canada.

The FTA origin rule provides an imperfect model for the NAFTA, but one that will be difficult to improve upon in the NAFTA negotiations. However, the FTA approach is complex; special sectoral rules provide a goldmine for accountants and lawyers. In some cases, firms have preferred to continue to pay MFN tariffs rather than undertake the paperwork necessary to qualify for FTA preferences.[18]

NAFTA origin rules are particularly important for the U.S. automobile and auto parts industries. These firms are prepared to contest the entire agreement if the restrictive local content rule that applies uniquely to this sector is lowered. Indeed, the U.S. firms want the requirement tightened so

16　Hart considers rules of origin "the most difficult and the most important chapter that will have to be tackled in negotiating Mexican accession." See Hart, Michael, *A North American Free Trade Agreement: The Strategic Implications for Canada*, Halifax, Nova Scotia: Institute for Research on Public Policy, 1990, p. 104.

17　That is why the general origin rule in the Canada-U.S. FTA is supplemented by numerous industry specific rules (usually of a more restrictive character) set out in the annex to FTA Chapter 3.

18　See Hart (1990), p. 106, and *Journal of Commerce*, 18 July 1991, p. 3A.

as to slow down the entry of new Japanese firms (beyond Nissan) into Mexico.[19]

Lipsey and Smith have argued that "the rules of origin for duty-free treatment within an FTA should be made more liberal as the external tariffs of the parties are reduced either on an MFN basis or through negotiations of further regional FTAs."[20] Following that logic, the enlargement of the FTA to include Mexico should lead to less restrictive origin rules in the NAFTA. However, we believe the NAFTA negotiators should simply adopt the existing FTA origin rules with as few sectoral exceptions as possible.[21]

Energy

The Canada-USA FTA already contains an extensive carve-out for energy industries from its investment provisions; Mexican officials will likely seek to extend the carve-out *inter alia* to the obligations regarding supply access assurances, so as to maintain as much flexibility as possible for national policies in this area.

To encourage the development of Mexican energy resources and to promote regional energy security, the United States may try to narrow the energy carve-out from existing FTA disciplines on investment. New investment in energy infrastructure (e.g., electricity grids; natural gas pipelines; oil refineries) is critical for both objectives. In this case, the Mexican and Canadian position is juxtaposed against that of the United States. However, Mexico needs to increase production in the energy sector to bolster growth prospects, and will need substantial foreign participation to fulfil Pemex's ambitious investment plans. The three countries will likely follow pragmatic detours around the sovereignty land mines buried in Mexico and Canada.

---

19 See Motor Vehicle Manufacturers Association, "Proposed Policy Positions for the Automotive Provisions of a North American Free Trade Agreement," paper submitted to the U.S. Trade Representative, 9 September 1991.

20 Lipsey, Richard G., and Murray G. Smith, "The Canada-US Free Trade Agreement: Special Case or Wave of the Future?" in Jeffrey J. Schott, ed., *Free Trade Areas and U.S. Trade Policy*, Washington, DC: Institute for International Economics, 1989, p. 328.

21 In Chapter 8, we recommend that the three countries rely on the general rule of origin set out in FTA Chapter 3, appropriately modified to address "roll-up" problems in the auto sector, and then rely on dispute resolution panels to devise sectoral exceptions when the general rules are abused.

Cultural Industries

FTA Article 2005 exempts specified cultural industries from most FTA obligations. As a result, trade and investment policies affecting particular goods and services (including *inter alia* the print media, film and music recordings, and radio and television broadcasts) can still discriminate against foreign suppliers. Nonetheless, a substantial share of Canadian sales of books, periodicals, and movies come from the United States.[22]

Canada considers Article 2005 critical to safeguard its "cultural sovereignty" and regards the FTA cultural exemptions as inviolate.[23] By contrast, the United States argues that the exemption should be narrowed to limit the scope of foreign investment restrictions and to allow the full exploitation of copyrights throughout the region. Mexico seems to be less sensitive than Canada to the need to protect "cultural" industries;[24] its main sovereignty concern involves the energy sector, as noted above. The diverse set of attitudes toward cultural questions suggests an outcome that entails separate schedules of specific national practices that are excepted from the general disciplines of NAFTA (following the FTA precedent).

NAFTA: Improving on the USA-Canada Model

What kind of animal will this NAFTA be? Until the Canadian decision to join the negotiating party in January 1991, the number of possible outcomes seemingly was limited only by the spirited imagination of trade negotiators.

As the talks began in June 1991, the form and substance of the NAFTA was still unclear. However, the number of options seemed to have been pared down to three: separate bilaterals subsumed under a trilateral

---

22 Ryan, Leo, "Canadian Culture Under Seige?" *Journal of Commerce*, 8 August 1991, p. 4A.

23 For a thorough discussion of the cultural sovereignty issue and Canadian concerns, see Carr, Graham, "Trade Liberalization and the Political Economy of Culture: An International Perspective on FTA," *Occasional Paper* 6, Bangor, ME: The Canadian-American Center at the University of Maine, 1991.

24 Jaime Serra Puche, the Mexican Secretary of Commerce, has made this point quite starkly: "The free trade agreement does not threaten the Mexican cultural identity" (as quoted in *El Nacional*, 21 June 1991, p. 2). Similarly, Herminio Blanco, Mexico's chief NAFTA negotiator, has declared that "the cultural industries have to be negotiated as part of the services sector, which includes entertainment" (as quoted in the *Journal of Commerce*, 8 August 1991, p. 9A).

umbrella; a hybrid between a bilateral and trilateral pact; or a trilateralization of a new, improved Canada-USA FTA.

Separate Bilateral FTAs

Until the Canadian decision to seek a trilateral pact, the negotiation of separate bilateral FTAs seemed to have been the *modus operandi* for crafting a NAFTA. The United States would negotiate an FTA with Mexico, effectively implementing a "hub-and-spoke" policy; Canada and Mexico could do the same, building on their March 1990 Framework Pacts; and over time the three separate bilateral FTAs then could be covered under a trilateral umbrella agreement.

As Ronald J. Wonnacott (1990) has pointed out, the United States would come out ahead of its FTA partners under a hub-and-spoke approach, since it would benefit from freer trade with both countries (which in turn would make it the preferred market for new investment), while Canada would face increased competition in the U.S. market and continued discrimination (compared to U.S. firms) in the Mexican market. Moreover, Canada would not have the opportunity to influence the terms of the USA-Mexico arrangement if it sat on the sidelines, even if Canada and Mexico worked out their own bilateral FTA. For those reasons among others, Canada opted to join the USA-Mexico talks. The separate bilateral option thus seems to have been relegated to a fallback role, in case the trilateral approach breaks down (or Canada backs out for domestic political reasons).

Hybrid Trilateral

The hybrid approach mixes trilateral obligations in a "core" agreement with separate bilateral commitments on specific issues. The larger the "core," the more this approach parallels the straight trilateralization option discussed below.

The hybrid approach would set out an umbrella agreement among the three countries that would establish common administrative and dispute settlement provisions, as well as commitments regarding trade liberalization. The existing Canada-USA FTA would remain intact. Each country would negotiate separate arrangements with Mexico regarding the extent to which Mexico would assume specific rights and obligations on goods, services, and perhaps investment and intellectual property; the schedule of those bilateral commitments would be annexed to the trilateral NAFTA framework.

Lipsey[25] favours a hybrid approach which combines a "core" agreement involving liberalization of trade in goods and services, as well as institutional provisions relating to dispute settlement and administration of the pact, with separate bilateral pacts between the partner countries. In essence, the "core" would be a diluted version of the Canada-USA FTA that would be applied in its entirety by all three countries.[26] The Canada-USA FTA would be preserved, and Mexico would negotiate side agreements with the United States and Canada to supplement its undertakings in areas not covered by the core agreement.

Trilateralization of the Canada-USA FTA

The most straightforward approach to a NAFTA would be simply to trilateralize the Canada-USA FTA by having Mexico accede to the existing agreement. Even better, all three countries could use the opportunity to improve the existing pact in the areas already noted. As a practical matter, some amendment would be necessary upon Mexican accession because several of the FTA provisions involve separate national obligations on specific issues and would thus require complementary commitments relating to Mexican policies. Striking examples include financial services, insurance, and agricultural reforms.

The straight trilateral approach could have some drawbacks, however. Both Hart (1990) and Lipsey (1991) have surveyed the provisions of the Canada-USA pact and found numerous areas where Mexico could have problems in accepting FTA obligations; the most prominent examples involve energy, government procurement, and dispute resolution provisions. Both Hart and Lipsey conclude that a hybrid approach to NAFTA would be more practical than the more ambitious trilateralization option.

However, their policy recommendation rests on two critical assumptions: that Mexico will only accept asymmetrical obligations because of its level of development; and that Mexico's different legal system will complicate the evolution of a common dispute settlement mechanism. On close examination, those assumptions do not stand up.

---

25   Lipsey, Richard G., "The Case for Trilateralism," in Steven Globerman, ed., *Continental Accord: North American Economic Integration*, Vancouver: Fraser Institute, 1991.

26   According to Lipsey, the Core Agreement would exclude FTA chapters 7 (agriculture), 9 (energy), 13 (government procurement), 16 (investment), and Article 2005 (cultural industries). See Lipsey, "The Case for Trilateralism," p. 114.

Symmetric Obligations

The first assumption implies that developing countries start, by definition, at a competitive disadvantage in an FTA and therefore need to maintain their trade barriers longer than their industrialized partners. Indeed, there are few instances in history where developed and developing countries joined in an FTA. This may partly reflect the self-fulfilling prophecy of protection: trade barriers are frequently so high in developing countries that many firms fear they can not survive the shock of adjustment to open competition with an industrial economy.

Mexico seems to be an exception to the historical LDC predilection for protection. The Mexican policy of *apertura* is based on a willing embrace of liberal trade and investment policies as the preferred path to economic growth. So far, the Mexican experiment has succeeded brilliantly: inflation has subsided, distortions have been reduced, the stock market is booming, and growth has resumed. But Mexico needs to sustain and augment its recent reforms to encourage the new investment required to finance development over the long haul. Accession to the full obligations of the NAFTA would continue and solidify the on-going reform process; differential and delayed staging of trade reforms would simply retard adjustment.[27]

That said, Mexico should be able to commit to reciprocal trade liberalization in the NAFTA. Mexico's average tariff is comparable to that of Canada prior to the introduction of the FTA reforms, and should be phased out in a similar ten-year time period.[28] Liberalization in the auto and petrochemical sectors will be more difficult, but the adjustment in Mexico should be facilitated by investment in new plant and equipment. In agriculture, the pace of reform will need to be slower, but even then Mexico should be able to keep up with the snail's pace of agricultural reform set out in the Canada-USA pact.

27 Indeed, Mexico needs to *avoid* differential treatment in all but extreme circumstances. Differential treatment is usually rationalized as a crutch to prop up a weak economy; often, however, it becomes a handicap because it poses a sugar-coated obstacle to adjustment.

28 As a result, Mexican imports would still be subject to some tariffs for a few years after the complete elimination of duties on U.S./Canadian trade. One would expect, however, that after the NAFTA is signed, the tariff cuts would be accelerated (as has occurred twice already in the USA-Canada context).

Of course, Mexico need not pursue identical obligations to those committed by Canada and the United States, but it should be able to eliminate its tariffs as well as most import licensing requirements in a comparable timeframe. Indeed, the United States and Canada may be more likely than Mexico to seek extended phase-out periods to ease the pain of reform in their most protected sectors (e.g., apparel; fruits and vegetables).

Mexico should be able to accept the full range of NAFTA obligations, including those pertaining to services, investment, and intellectual property (and, indeed, should accede to the accords under negotiation in the Uruguay Round). Mexico has already undertaken significant reforms (most recently with regard to protection of intellectual property) that are bringing many of its domestic regulations into conformity with the standards of the United States and other OECD countries.[29]

Furthermore, Mexico should be able to sign all of the GATT codes on nontariff barriers,[30] and align its domestic procedures to the international norms established by those agreements (including antidumping, where despite being a signatory to the GATT code, Mexican administrative practices remain somewhat arbitrary). Such action would make Mexican administrative procedures more transparent and consistent with U.S. and Canadian norms, and establish a common basis for the review of antidumping and countervailing duty actions required to implement FTA Chapter 19 procedures. Mexico's willingness to sign the GATT codes, or to extend comparable rights to its NAFTA partners, should be a prerequisite for the inclusion of FTA chapters 18 and 19 dispute resolution procedures in the NAFTA. There is little reason to doubt that Mexico will do so. Thus, the legal differences between NAFTA partners may not be as hard to bridge as Hart and Lipsey imagine.

Dispute Settlement in the NAFTA

The dispute settlement mechanisms in FTA chapters 18 and 19 are among the most important benefits conferred by the FTA. For Canada, they provide an important binational check on the abuse of U.S. trade laws. For the same reason, Mexico would like comparable provisions in the NAFTA.

---

29 Moreover, Mexico is now seeking membership in the OECD to reinforce and further extend its economic reforms.

30 Mexico is not yet a signatory to the GATT subsidies and government procurement codes. It signed the licensing, customs valuation, and antidumping codes in July 1987, and the standards code in January 1988 (USITC 1990, 2-3).

Canada is wary that a trilateralization of the dispute settlement process could dilute its "positive" influence on U.S. trade policies. Furthermore, both the United States and Canada are concerned that Mexico's different legal system and traditions will impede the enforcement of NAFTA rules. The Canada-USA FTA contains a bifurcated dispute settlement process. In most areas, disputes between the FTA partners are reviewed under the general procedures of FTA Chapter 18. However, disputes concerning antidumping and countervailing duties, which have accounted for the vast majority of cases brought under the FTA, are handled under the provisions of FTA Chapter 19.[31]

FTA Chapter 18 establishes an alternative to GATT dispute settlement procedures (although both countries reserve their right to take cases to the GATT). Disputes raised by either country are examined by a panel of experts that follow procedures adopted from U.S.-Canadian legal experience. As in the GATT, findings of expert panels are subject to review by a senior political body (the Canada-United States Trade Commission).

By contrast, disputes brought under Chapter 19 procedures are subject to binding panel rulings. Jean Anderson[32] succinctly describes the function of a dispute panel under Chapter 19 of the Canada-USA FTA: "the panel is to review a final determination, based on the administrative record, to determine whether the determination was in accordance with the AD or CVD law of the importing country, and must apply the standard of review and general legal principles of the importing country." In essence, FTA panels *substitute* for judicial review of trade actions. The fact that Mexico's nascent antidumping regime has not yet established a track record of judicial review is thus less troublesome, since NAFTA provisions make that process redundant.[33]

By all accounts, the FTA dispute settlement process has worked exceedingly well. Only two cases have been reviewed under the general

---

31 Neither process applies to disputes over financial services, which are handled separately by the U.S. Treasury and the Canadian Department of Finance according to the provisions of FTA Chapter 17.

32 Anderson, Jean, "Resolving Trade Disputes through Binational Panels and Extraordinary Challenges: Issues in Implementing Chapter 19 of the Canada-United States Free Trade Agreement," in Richard G. Dearden, Michael M. Hart, and Debra P. Steger, eds., *Living with Free Trade: Canada, the Free Trade Agreement and the GATT*, Halifax, Nova Scotia: Institute for Research on Public Policy, 1989, p. 15.

33 The U.S. Trade Agreements Act of 1979 first authorized judicial review of CVD and ADD cases, so the U.S. track record for such reviews is not that long either.

procedures of Chapter 18.[34] By contrast, as of June 1991, fifteen cases had been brought under Chapter 19, of which seven were settled, three terminated, two consolidated with another panel, and three were pending. In almost every case, the strict time limits of the FTA process have been kept. Panels have not acted as rubber stamps for national regulators; instead, some national actions have been overturned. Moreover, the decision by an extraordinary challenge committee to uphold the panel findings in the most contentious case to date--a dispute involving Canadian pork subsidies-- seems to have bolstered the credibility of the FTA process.[35]

If Mexico aligns its administrative procedures to U.S. and Canadian norms in terms of open proceedings and written opinions,[36] there should be no serious problem with regard to Mexican participation in dispute resolution provisions under the NAFTA. Mexican application of the general obligations of the NAFTA could be resolved in the context of a regional dispute settlement mechanism, modelled on FTA Chapter 18 procedures. Panellists should continue to be drawn from the disputing parties, but the panel chairman should be selected from the third country. If all three countries are involved in a dispute, each should be represented and the three should then select a fourth as chairman.

Trilateralization of the Chapter 19 process entails a few more complications, although none are insurmountable. The key concern involves Mexico's often opaque administrative procedures. Transparency can be achieved by Mexican adoption of the procedural obligations of the GATT Code on Subsidies and Countervailing Measures, and the GATT Code on Antidumping. NAFTA panels could then function in the same manner, and

---

34 Both cases were brought in 1989: Pacific Coast Salmon and Herring; and Lobsters.

35 Bello, Holmer, and Kelly (1991) provide a good summary of each case brought under Chapter 18 (general cases) and Chapter 19 (subsidies and antidumping). See Bello, Judith H., Alan F. Holmer, and Debra A. Kelly, "Midterm Report on Binational Dispute Settlement Under the United States-Canada Free-Trade Agreement," *The International Lawyer*, Vol. 25, No. 2, 1991. For a report on the panel decision that ordered the rescission of US countervailing duties on Canadian pork, also see *International Trade Reporter*, 19 June 1991, p. 933.

36 US and Canadian negotiators have rightly argued that without these changes, the FTA Chapter 19 procedures would be unworkable with regard to Mexican cases.

subject to comparable procedures, as in the FTA.[37] In sum, the FTA Chapter 19 process has worked surprisingly well for the United States and Canada, and should be carried over into the NAFTA.[38]

Future Expansion of the FTA

When the United States and Canada negotiated their FTA, the question of whether the agreement would be extended to third countries was more theoretical than real. Mexico was seen as a distant candidate; the pertinent issue seemed to be whether the FTA would be a building block for broader multilateral accords in the GATT or would be emulated by other countries in the event that the Uruguay Round faltered.[39] Moreover, U.S. fast track procedures were designed to accommodate either bilateral FTAs or a multilateral trade pact in the GATT; they did not easily accommodate the notification of trilateral talks.[40]

Today, the prospect of future expansion of the NAFTA, or at least of additional FTAs between the United States and other countries, is enshrined in the Enterprise for the Americas Initiative (EAI). The United States has committed to negotiate FTAs with other countries in Latin America after the conclusion of trade talks with Mexico and Canada. The decision as to whether those negotiations will be conducted with individual countries or with groups of countries (such as the Andean Pact and Mercosur) is as yet unsettled. To be eligible for FTA talks, however, U.S. officials have

---

37 Concerns about the lack of legal experience of Mexican panellists with these procedures seem to be exaggerated. Mexico has many fine jurists (often schooled in the best U.S. and Canadian law schools); panellists need not be lawyers (indeed, economists deserve more representation on panels); and Mexican officials already have experience with international dispute settlement processes.

38 This conclusion is reinforced if substantive agreements are eventually reached in the NAFTA on subsidies and countervailing duties and on antidumping rules. Even with NAFTA accords, initial decisions would presumably still be made by national authorities. Hence, there would be plenty of room for resort to a trilateral appeals process.

39 Jeffrey J. Schott, ed., *Free Trade Areas and U.S. Trade Policy*, Washington, DC: Institute for International Economics, 1989.

40 To be on the safe side, U.S. officials notified their intent to use fast track authorities for trilateral negotiations in February 1991, thus providing the House Ways and Means and Senate Finance Committees an additional 60 legislative days to approve or deny the request. At that time, the 60-day period was about to expire for a similar notification that had been made in September 1990 with regard to bilateral talks with Mexico.

indicated that a candidate country should be "committed to a stable macroeconomic environment and market-oriented policies" and should be making "progress in achieving open trade regimes."[41] The focus should be on recent trends rather than historical precedents.[42]

The hub-and-spoke issue thus again confronts Canada and Mexico, even as NAFTA negotiations just begin. Both countries are likely to insist that the NAFTA include provisions regarding how to deal with prospective new FTA partners. Three options seem feasible: adding an accession clause to the NAFTA; negotiating FTAs between the NAFTA countries as a whole and other countries; or simply invoking consultation clauses in the NAFTA to ensure that Canadian and Mexican interests are not impaired as a result of U.S. negotiations with other countries in the region.[43]

The first option--an accession clause--is modelled after current GATT practice and the accession of new members to the European Community.[44] Prospective new entrants would apply for accession to the NAFTA, and negotiate their entry terms with the existing membership. They would assume all the obligations of the NAFTA, except as specified in their protocol of accession (which would set the timetable for coming into conformity with NAFTA rules and agreed reservations).[45] Acceptance of the terms of the protocol would be by consensus of the existing members.

The second option--joint negotiations--is a variant of the first. It would require the formation of a joint NAFTA negotiating team comprised of U.S., Canadian, and Mexican officials to work out the terms of a new FTA between the NAFTA members and the candidate country or group of countries. Such an accord would be much less comprehensive than the

---

41   Katz, Julius L., Testimony before the Committee on Finance, United States Senate, on the Enterprise for the Americas Initiative, April 24 1991, pp. 7-8.

42   Hufbauer, Gary Clyde, and Jeffrey J. Schott, "Reaching for the Stars," *Latin Finance*, March 1991, p. 52, set out five preconditions for free trade talks: monetary stability, market-oriented policies, reduced budgetary reliance on import and export taxes, strong trade linkages, and functioning democracies.

43   Of course, this provision would also apply to bilateral or plurilateral FTA negotiations conducted by Mexico or Canada.

44   This is sometimes referred to as a "docking" clause.

45   These protocols would also be subject to review under the provisions of GATT Article XXIV to ensure that the interests of nonmember countries are not adversely affected by the FTA trade preferences.

NAFTA, perhaps covering only "traditional" trade issues such as tariffs, quotas, and licensing practices (otherwise it would make more sense to negotiate a protocol of accession to the NAFTA itself).

The third option--a consultation clause--presents the path of least resistance for the current NAFTA negotiators. It assumes that the United States will receive the bulk of requests for new FTAs,[46] and provides a mechanism for Mexico and Canada to keep informed on those prospective negotiations so that they can consult about issues that affect their economic interests. It does not resolve the hub-and-spoke dilemma for Canada and Mexico, but it makes the process more transparent and tolerable.

Of the three options, the accession clause is by far the most desirable. It encourages other countries in the region to continue to pursue trade and investment reforms so that they will be eligible to join the NAFTA; and it provides the opportunity to build a common regime and thus avoid the patchwork quilt of trade arrangements that could arise if all three countries negotiate separately and establish different accords with third countries.

The main problem with an accession clause is whether the United States will be able to accept new members without new authority from the Congress, since current U.S. law bars the extension of FTA benefits to third countries. If an accession clause were included in the NAFTA and accepted by Congress in the NAFTA implementing legislation, there would seem to be no need for Congressional approval of additional membership applications.[47] However, Congress is likely to want a bite at the apple each time a new member applies for NAFTA membership.

To address Congressional concerns, the NAFTA should include a "non-application provision," akin to GATT Article XXXV, that allows countries to deny the extension of the benefits of the NAFTA to any new member at the time of its accession. Under this provision, the President would seek Congressional approval of new members under fast track provisions, and invoke the non-application provision if the Congress disapproved. As a practical matter, the United States would probably substantially influence the terms of the protocol of accession of new members (as it did with the

---

46 However, the consultation process would not necessarily be a one-way street to Washington. Mexico is already negotiating FTAs and preferential trading arrangements with other countries in the Western Hemisphere, including Chile, Venezuela, and the Central American nations.

47 Accession clauses are common in *multilateral* agreements; Congress does not act when new signatories accede to the GATT or the GATT codes negotiated during the Tokyo Round.

Mexican protocol of accession to the GATT), and thereby seek to assuage specific Congressional concerns *before* an applicant entered the club. Of course, other NAFTA members could also invoke that provision.

Which countries should be eligible for membership in the NAFTA? In principle, if Canada, Mexico and the United States are truly multilateral in outlook, accession would be open to any GATT member. The process of regional liberalization could thus be extended to a broader group of countries--and the more countries that join, the closer regional liberalization would come to parallel global liberalization.[48]

As a practical matter, however, membership should initially be limited to the Western Hemisphere. This constraint would serve two purposes: first, it would set geographical boundaries on the NAFTA and thus follow GATT practice, if not law, in accepting FTAs under GATT Article XXIV;[49] and second, it would avoid complications that could arise if countries sought to include restrictive provisions in the NAFTA to guard against the future accession of East Asian trading powers, for example.

Over the medium to long term, the enlargement of NAFTA will depend importantly on the pace of multilateral trade liberalization in the GATT. The NAFTA should serve as a catalyst for continued trade and investment reforms in the Western Hemisphere and thus reinforce efforts to that end in the GATT. If the Uruguay Round comes up short, however, the NAFTA could become a "GATT-Plus" agreement (as originally envisaged in the 1970s) that commits its members to broader rights and obligations than existing GATT provisions. Under those conditions, there is no reason to restrict the geographic reach of the membership, which could then be open to all GATT members.[50]

---

48   For a broader discussion of this general point, see Hufbauer, Gary Clyde, *The Free Trade Debate*, Report of the Twentieth Century Fund Task Force on the Future of American Trade Policy, New York, NY: Priority Press, 1989 and *Financial Times*, "Trading blocs and the GATT," 14 June 1991, p. 18.

49   GATT Article XXIV does not contain a geographical proximity test, but almost all FTAs and customs unions that have been reviewed under its provisions (including the EC) have limited membership to the immediate neighbourhood.

50   Given their reactions to NAFTA so far, several East Asian countries may well be interested in joining a "GATT-Plus" club, if the GATT process faltered. In that event, NAFTA could serve as a model both for the Enterprise Initiative in the Western Hemisphere and for closer trade relations among countries in the Pacific Basin.

Annex A: NAFTA Negotiating Groups

1. Market Access
   a) Tariffs and nontariff barriers
   b) Rules of origin
   c) Government procurement
   d) Agriculture
   e) Automobiles
   f) Other industrial sectors
      i) Textiles
      ii) Energy
2. Trade Rules
   a) Safeguards
   b) Subsidies; Countervailing and antidumping duties
   c) Standards
      i) Health and safety
      ii) Industrial
3. Services
   a) Principles of services
   b) Financial
   c) Insurance
   d) Land transportation
   e) Telecommunications
   f) Other services
4. Investment (principles and restrictions)
5. Intellectual Property
6. Dispute Settlement

Chapter 4

Transition Mechanisms and Safeguards in a North American Free Trade Agreement

Peter Morici

Introduction

A free trade agreement with Mexico offers the United States and Canada important opportunities. The combination of Mexican labour and U.S. and Canadian capital and technology would help all three North American economies counter the enhanced competitive capabilities Japan enjoys through its expansion of trade and investment in East and Southeast Asia and the European Community (EC) should obtain through enhanced commercial ties with the liberalizing economies of Eastern Europe. By fostering a more efficient allocation of continental resources and attracting additional overseas capital and technology, free trade should improve the international competitiveness of all three North American economies.

The Importance of Adjustment

Adjustment is essential to achieving these gains.

In Mexico, the traditional manufacturing sector[1] must modernize to successfully service a continental market in some industries and contract to

---

1   In this paper, the term "traditional manufacturing sector" is used to refer to the non-Maquiladora manufacturing sector. This traditional sector, which developed behind a highly protective structure of tariffs, quotas and nontariff barriers, accounts for less than one-half of Mexico's manufactured exports.

make way for more competitive U.S. and Canadian products in others. Even in Mexican industries with strong export prospects, substantial intraindustry adjustments may be expected, because the firms that serviced the Mexican market under the pre-1985 import-substitution regime will not always be the ones capable of creating new, more competitive facilities. Nevertheless, if this process is successful, Mexico will gain a modern, sophisticated and efficient manufacturing sector, and real incomes will rise.

In the United States and Canada, jobs in low- and medium-technology activities must make way for jobs in high-technology activities. Generally, this will entail the loss of low-skill/wage jobs in industries such as consumer electronics and the gain of high-skill/wage jobs in industries such as advanced telecommunications equipment. However, in some low- and medium-technology activities with strong unions (e.g., certain automotive components and assembly) high paying factory jobs will be lost too. Overall, this process should permit U.S. and Canadian firms to keep the production of some products in North America that would have moved to East and Southeast Asia or elsewhere.

Japan, through its expansion of trade and investment in East and Southeast Asia, is systematically exporting low-technology/skill/wage industries and increasing its emphasis on high-technology/skill/wage activities. For Germany and other Northern European countries, the opening of Eastern Europe presents similar opportunities.

If the United States and Canada successfully make the same kind of adjustments, they will emerge more competitive vis-à-vis Japan and the EC and with higher real incomes. However, reports of inadequate entry-level skills among U.S. high school graduates indicate that transition will be impeded by skill shortages and that the distributional effects of free trade could be more significant than has heretofore been anticipated (discussed below).

The skills issue aside, these kinds of labour market adjustments can be painful and the costs imposed on workers and communities required to find new employers will rise with the amount of resource reallocation motivated by free trade. Similarly, the gains from free trade also rise with the amount of resource reallocation precipitated by the removal of artificial impediments to continental trade and investment flows. Other things equal, the pain imposed by continental free trade will rise with the gains.

The Role of Transition Mechanisms

How acute is this relationship? That depends on how efficiently markets are able to reallocate capital and retrain labour, and how much additional foreign investment is attracted to a more dynamic and healthier North American economy created by free trade.

During any time span, the capacities of individual markets and their participants to adjust to the shocks imposed by trade liberalization, or similar exogenous changes in public policy, are limited. The gains from a specific set of trade liberalization measures may be maximized and the underemployment of resources minimized by phasing out tariffs and other trade barriers at rates consistent with the adjustment capabilities of firms and workers in individuals markets. This is why, for example, eliminating some tariffs immediately while phasing out others over five or ten years in the Canada-USA Free Trade Agreement (FTA) was sound economics, as well as good politics.

This said, policymakers should be encouraged to recognize that the optimal path from a more protected economy to a more open and efficient economy generally entails some dislocations and temporary underemployment of resources. In considering alternative transition mechanisms and schedules, it is important for negotiators (and the economists that advise them) to weigh the costs of short-term underemployment against the discounted present value of the gains from freer trade.

Such evaluations can never be precise, and in the end, the political leverage of affected workers and firms significantly affects the rates of discount politicians apply in their assessments of the needs of particular industries. Higher rates of discount are almost always applied in large and/or geographically-dispersed[2] industries with powerful unions. Moreover, politicians invariably require that trade agreements include escape hatches or safeguard mechanisms for situations in which the adjustments imposed by trade liberalization are greater than anticipated or politically acceptable.

Unfortunately, safeguard mechanisms often have been misused. In the General Agreement on Tariffs and Trade (GATT), Article XIX was originally intended to ease adjustments in situations in which import surges followed closely on the heels of multilateral tariff reductions. It was not intended for situations in which other factors--for example, shifts in fundamental determinants of international cost advantages--were the primary impetus for import surges disrupting domestic markets. However, gradually, the attention paid to the distinction between import surges having their

---

2   Geographically dispersed industries enjoy the advantage of wider representation in legislative bodies. In the United States, this is particularly important in the Senate.

origins in recent tariff cuts and those emanating from other sources has diminished, and safeguard actions have been taken in response to autonomous changes in comparative advantages.

This lack of discipline has been apparent in other abuses, including the outright avoidance of Article XIX constraints through the use of grey-area measures (e.g., voluntary restraint agreements); the misuse of otherwise GATT-sanctioned trade remedies (e.g., dumping duties); and the all too frequent reliance on these kinds of practices to avoid or postpone inevitable adjustments.

Overall, this lack of discipline has been identified as a fundamental threat to the integrity of an open trading system under the GATT and has been the focus of intense negotiations in the Uruguay Round.

Focusing on the United States, safeguard actions have been taken in situations in which recent tariff reductions have not been the primary cause of import surges disrupting domestic markets--consider specialty steel in the 1980s. Where safeguard actions have proved inconvenient or insufficient, extra-GATT mechanisms have been used--consider the U.S. "success" with the Multifiber Agreement and voluntary restraint agreements (VRAs) for automobiles and steel. In apparel and steel, it is difficult to argue that U.S. policy has facilitated an orderly movement of resources to other, more efficient, pursuits.

If we are to learn from these mistakes, we must embody in a trilateral agreement transition mechanisms and safeguards that ensure that adjustments take place. Only in this way will markets, not politics, determine where many products are made. However, if good economics is to prevail over bad politics, then negotiators, and the economists that advise them, should recognize some important political and economic realities about establishing a single North American market.

Maintaining Political Support for Trade Liberalization

First, the articulation and implementation of a free trade agreement with Mexico will extend many years beyond the fast track negotiations and the inauguration of the initial agreement. If a trilateral accord is to initiate a process of fully integrating the three North American economies, then it must engage the three national governments in a long and detailed process of follow-on negotiations in which concessions, well beyond the phased elimination of tariffs and quantitative restrictions, are exchanged over many years.[3] Therefore, for the full promise of a modern trade agreement to be fulfilled, political support for liberalization must be sustained for many years. The size and perceived source of trade-related labour market adjustments are critical in this regard.

As discussed in Section I, the U.S. labour adjustments perceived to be associated with a free trade agreement with Mexico may prove much larger than the careful economic analyses undertaken to date indicate. Generally the latter have focused on remaining Mexican tariffs and quantitative restrictions; however, other factors will contribute to adjustments, and some may be determined to flow from the environment created by free trade. These include the yet to be realized consequences of economic reforms in Mexico, changes in incentives for the managers of Maquiladoras under free trade, intraindustry adjustments that are partially missed by even significantly disaggregated models, and competitive weaknesses in the U.S. and Canadian economies that will be exacerbated by free trade.

We can debate whether all of these would be the consequence of free trade. For example, is free trade necessary to sustain economic reform in Mexico? If so, many of the competitive consequences of Mexican reform for U.S. and Canadian workers could be attributed to free trade. If not, then these competitive consequences should not be attributed to free trade. Unfortunately, economics does not provide tools to resolve such issues.

Such uncertainties notwithstanding, history has taught us that the political process does not distinguish well between the labour market disruptions imposed by imports resulting from recent tariff cuts and those changes in the trading environment unrelated to recent actions taken under trade agreements.

If a trade agreement does not adequately address the labour adjustment costs created by increased imports from Mexico, regardless of whether they result from the elimination of tariffs and other actions independent of the free trade agreement, experiences with multilateral liberalization indicates that political pressures will mount on the President and the Congress to take

---

3   One of the more powerful lessons of the 1987-1988 U.S.-Canada talks was that fast-track negotiations was only the first step in a protracted and complicated process. For example, the FTA commits the United States and Canada to negotiations regarding standards and technical regulations, an open border for agricultural products and inputs, domestic subsidies and countervailing duties, cross-border dumping and domestic predatory pricing, procurement, professional licensing and the regulation of business services, automotive policies, and many other issues. The breadth of this agenda rivals the European Community 1992 program.

protectionist steps. In the end, political support for adherence to the disciplines of the agreement and follow-on negotiations could dissolve.

Assessing the Scope of the Adjustment Costs

Most economic studies estimate the benefits and adjustment costs of a free trade agreement for the United States to be small, because the Mexican economy is quite small relative to the U.S. economy and both countries have already substantially reduced their trade barriers.[4] For example, the KPMG Peat Marwick Computational General Equilibrium model estimates that eliminating tariffs and various quantitative restrictions would raise GNP by 0.04 percent in the United States and 0.32 percent in Mexico. Other models yield similarly small results.[5]

---

4   By the end of 1990, U.S. and Mexican tariffs in bilateral trade averaged 6 and 11 percent. The United States applied quantitative restrictions on textiles, apparel, steel, and a few agricultural commodities, and Mexico required import licenses for about 20 percent of tariff items. See KPMG Peat Marwick Policy Economics Group, *The Effects of a Free Trade Agreement Between the U.S. and Mexico*, New York: 1991; and U.S. International Trade Commission, *The Likely Impact on the United States of a Free Trade Agreement with Mexico*, Report No. 2352, February 1991.

5   For example, an INFORUM study estimates that free trade would increase U.S. GNP 2/10s of 1 percent and lower Mexican GNP 3/10s of 1 percent. It would increase U.S. imports and exports by 0.4 and 1.6 percent and increase Mexican imports and exports by 4.1 percent and 20 percent. In the United States, the apparel industry would lose the most jobs--about 7200 or less than 1 percent of 1989 employment.

   Similarly, the International Trade Commission concluded that the likely benefits to the U.S. economy and net effects on individual sectors of the economy would be modest. According to the ITC study:

>   The results of the Commission's analysis show that an FTA with Mexico may have moderate to significant effects on U.S. trade with Mexico in many of the industries covered [in this report]. However, these trade gains or losses, though considerable, ... would likely have a negligible impact on production levels in most of the U.S. industries, both overall and regionally. This is because the expected gains and losses in U.S. trade with Mexico would represent a very small share of these industries' domestic production.

   The Berkeley and University of Michigan models reached similar conclusions.

   See KPMG Peat Marwick Policy Economics Group, *The Effects of a Free Trade Agreement Between the U.S. and Mexico*; INFORUM, *Industrial Effects of a Free Trade Agreement Between Mexico and the USA*, College Park, MD: March 5, 1991; U.S. International Trade Commission, *The Likely Impact on the United States of a Free Trade Agreement with Mexico*; Hinojosa-Ojeda, Raul, and Sherman Robinson, "Alternative

(continued...)

If it is further and optimistically assumed that free trade induces $25 billion in additional investment in Mexico (i.e., 7.6 percent of Mexico's capital stock and enough to keep the cost of capital from rising[6]), 40 percent of this capital comes from foreign investors and 60 percent from domestic sources, and the additional foreign investment in Mexico has no effect on domestic investment in the United States (all additional U.S. investment is diverted from other foreign projects), then the Peat Marwick model estimates that free trade raises real incomes in the United States and Mexico by 0.04 and 6.6 percent, respectively, after long term adjustments have occurred.[7] Under this scenario the largest negative employment effects in the United States are in electronics and apparel; these sectors lose 4,700 and 4,400 jobs, respectively, or less than one percent of their total employment. Sugar refining is the only sector estimated to lose more than one percent of its employment--2.4 percent or 1,700.

If the anticipated benefits from free trade are indeed modest, it should be asked why the Bush and Salinas administrations are willing to go to such great lengths to achieve free trade in the first place? The answer is that the benefits and costs for the Mexican and U.S. economies should be larger than these studies indicate for several reasons.

First, we have yet to see the full impacts of Mexico's economic reform program on its industrial structure and export capacity.

Although about 45 percent of Mexico's exports to the United States enter at reduced rates of duty through the Maquiladora program, it is important to recognize that the Maquiladoras did not become so important in the Mexican export equation because U.S. barriers to other Mexican exports were so high. Rather, the Maquiladora's became important because the development of export-oriented production in the traditional Mexican economy was blocked by aggressive industrial policies emphasizing import-substitution. Historically, the greatest impediments to Mexican exports have

---

5(...continued)

Scenarios of U.S.-Mexico Integration: A Computational General Equilibrium Approach," Working Papers No. 609, Berkeley Department of Agricultural and Resource Economics, University of California at Berkeley; and Brown, Drusilla K., Alan V. Deardorff, and Robert B. Stern, "A North American Free Trade Agreement: Analytical Issues and a Computational Assessment," *The World Economy* (forthcoming).

6   Wage rates are constant in the KPMG Peat Marwick model.

7   The Berkeley model generates quite similar results for this scenario. GNP in the United States and Mexico rise by 0.1 and 6.4 percent. If additional capital investment in Mexico is halved, the results from the Berkeley model fall to 0.1 and 3.0.

not been U.S. tariffs and nontariff barriers but the constraints and inefficiencies imposed by decades of excessive regulation of private transactions, nationalist industrial policies and foreign perceptions of the insecurity of property rights.[8] The policies and their effects cannot be undone in six years.

In the 1980s, most new foreign investment in Mexico has been American and concentrated in the Maquiladora sector. Third-country investors, as well as Mexicans who took capital out of the country in the early 1980s, have been concerned about the durability of recent reforms and reluctant to invest in the traditional manufacturing sector. The "announcement effect" of free trade would likely assuage these concerns and accelerate U.S., Japanese and European investment and encourage the return of "flight capital."

Indeed, an important motivation for President Salinas in seeking free trade is to lock-in his reforms[9] and reassure and attract foreign investors. We are starting to see evidence of the efficacy of this strategy, as the mere announcement of negotiations and expectation of a free trade agreement is beginning to attract some formerly reluctant investors.[10]

Hence, assessments of free trade that only quantify the effects of the tariffs and quantitative restrictions remaining on paper miss many of the benefits and adjustments that continue to occur and would grow in intensity should a free trade agreement memorialize recent Mexican reforms, facilitate additional ones and positively influence the expectations and actions of foreign investors.

Second, focusing on the Maquiladoras, the managers of these mostly U.S. plants currently have strong incentives to import parts from the United States. In particular, when Maquiladora products are imported into the United States, duty is only charged on Mexican value added and components purchased from third countries. No duty is charged on components purchased in the United States. This incentive to choose U.S.

---

8   These perceptions were propagated by actions such as the nationalization of commercial banking in 1982 and the outright revocation of patent protection for many products in 1976.

9   The thinking is that once Mexico's commitment to reforms become part of an agreement or treaty with the United States future Mexican governments will find these reforms much more difficult to reverse.

10   Moffett, Matt, "Long Sickly Mexico Has Investment Boom As Trade Hopes Grow," *Wall Street Journal,* May 24, 1991, pp. A1, A4.

components over Mexican or third country components would disappear with the elimination of U.S. tariffs, and managers would be more likely to source in Asia and Europe when lower-cost components are available outside North America.

Third, although the effects of free trade on overall U.S., Canadian and Mexican agriculture and manufacturing may be small, and the same may be true for two- and three-digit industries, many of the adjustments will be intraindustry in scope. For example, in the electronics sector, the assembly of fairly standardized items will continue to move to Mexico, and Mexico will continue to expand its purchases of more sophisticated U.S. and Canadian telecommunications equipment. A similar process of intraindustry specialization may be expected in apparel, with Mexico making more lower-cost ties, shirts and pants, and the United States exporting knitwear, piece-goods and higher-valued fashion items. The net effect on U.S. and Canadian employment in the electrical equipment and apparel sectors will be smaller than on particular segments of the industry. Unfortunately, the jobs gained and lost often are not in the same locations, and by the very nature of increasing specialization--swapping low-skill/wage jobs for high-skill/wage jobs--employment consequences for different groups of workers are uneven.

Fourth, after free trade institutionalizes Mexican economic reforms, Japanese and European MNCs--often having better access to skilled labour, technology and capital than American and Canadian firms--may be in a better position to exploit new opportunities in Mexico than U.S. and Canadian MNCs. As a result, Mexican purchases of capital goods and services, which are now decidedly oriented toward the United States, could shift somewhat toward Japan and Europe.

For example, most Japanese automakers are in a better cash position and enjoy access to superior manufacturing technologies than their U.S. competitors. Mexico, through investments by Japanese automakers, could end up importing from Japan machine tools and advanced automotive components and exporting more low- and medium-technology components and assemblies and completed vehicles to the United States.

Certainly, U.S. suppliers would have some advantages in the Mexican market as a result of tariff-free access, but Mexican tariffs are no longer high enough to make a profound difference in the purchasing patterns of Japanese and EC MNCs, who, like their U.S. brethren, often prefer traditional suppliers.

Many analysts argue that strict rules of origin would be adequate to minimize such problems.[11] For example, a 50 or 60 percent North American content could be required. However, it is important to recognize that the bite of such rules would be directly related to the height of U.S. and Canadian most-favoured-nation (MFN) tariffs. Except in a few products, these tariffs are now quite low and are no longer principal impediments to Mexican exports. Moreover, rules of origin have no effect on purchases of capital equipment.[12]

Economists could argue that should a trade agreement with Mexico increase imports more than exports *ex ante*, the increase in the U.S. trade deficit would be corrected *ex post* by other market adjustments--especially, through exchange rate depreciation and changes in domestic relative prices and wages.[13] These would improve the price of competitiveness of U.S. industries seeking to export high-technology/skill products and U.S. import-competing industries making low- and medium-technology/skill products. However, we must ask ourselves towards what kinds of industries those adjustments would be skewed? Market adjustments could compel American firms and workers to place greater emphasis on less technology/skill-intensive activities that pay lower wages. This would greatly exacerbate downward pressure on the overall level of industrial wages.

The outcome will depend heavily on where young U.S. industrial workers' skills stand on the spectrum between Japanese and Western European workers, on the one hand, and Mexican industrial workers, on the other hand. The closer they are to the Mexicans, the more free trade induced adjustments could push them into competing with Mexicans for low-skilled jobs through lower wages and the less free trade would cause young industrial workers to specialize and compete with Japanese and European workers for high-skilled, high-wage jobs. In this context we should consider the following.

· The National Assessment of Educational Progress found that only 5 to 8 percent of all 17-year old American high school children

---

11 For example see U.S. International Trade Commission, *The Likely Impact on the United States of a Free Trade Agreement with Mexico*, pp. 2-5.

12 The value added created by capital equipment is treated as "domestic content."

13 The overall size of the U.S. trade deficit is determined by savings and investment imbalances between the United States and its principal trading partners. High Japanese savings rates, low U.S. savings rates and high U.S. federal budget deficits are major variables in this equation.

demonstrate the skills needed to function in demanding jobs or to do college work.[14]

- A large and growing body of evidence indicates that U.S. high school students are receiving educations that are inferior to those received by their peers in Japan and Western Europe. For example, in math and science, U.S. high school students lag Japanese students by more than 4 grade levels.[15]

- By some estimates about one in five Americans now hired is functionally illiterate (and innumerate), implying a U.S. literacy rate of 80 percent.[16]

- Mexico claims a literacy rate greater than 80 percent.[17]

Indeed, it bears mentioning, that substantial evidence is emerging that the majority of U.S. manufacturers, when they face new competitive pressures from low-wage imports, are forced by shortages of adequately educated and motivated industrial workers to deskill jobs and rely more on lower-wage, transient labour rather than to choose technology-intensive options and invest in training workers with requisite general education backgrounds.[18] Additional import competition from Mexico would intensify pressures on employers to deskill jobs and rely more on low-wage, transient workers.

14 Educational Testing Service, *America's Challenge: Accelerating Academic Achievement*, Princeton: Educational Testing Service, 1990.

15 See Commission on the Skills of the American Workforce, *America's Choice: high skills or low wages!* Rochester, NY: National Center on Education and the Economy, 1990; and Bishop, John, "Incentives for Learning: Why American High School Students Compare Poorly to Their Counterparts Overseas," Center for Advanced Human Resources Studies Working Paper 89-09, Ithaca: Cornell University, 1989.

16 Up to 65 percent of the U.S. workforce is "intermediary" literate--i.e., they can only read between the fifth and ninth grade levels. See Richards, Bill, "Wanting Workers: Just as jobs are demanding more, applicants are providing less," *Wall Street Journal*, February 9, 1990, p. R10; and Charlier, Marj, "Back to Basics: Businesses try to teach their workers the three R's since schools have failed to do so," *Wall Street Journal*, February 9, 1990, p. R14.

17 Committee for the Promotion of Investment in Mexico, *Mexico: Economic and Business Overview*, Mexico City: June 1990, p. 23.

18 Specifically, the reader is referred to the careful analysis reported in Commission on the Skills of the American Workforce, *America's Choice: high skills or low wages!*

The prominence of such a dynamic in the U.S. labour market and the potential for free trade to exacerbate its effects on the living standards of the average industrial worker in the United States does not imply that free trade will not generate aggregate benefits that exceed aggregate costs--the gains will exceed pain and by much more than economic studies to date indicate. However, the presence of such a dynamic does indicate that free trade will exacerbate the trend towards a less equal distribution of income.

While economists and other proponents of free trade can correctly counter that these are the fortunes of open competition, they should pause to consider the political consequences of such a dynamic for their long-term goal of creating a single North American market.

As noted in the introduction, creating a single North American market will require negotiations and exchanges of concessions over many years. If a free trade agreement does not handle adjustments properly, then nontariff concessions may never materialize from follow-on negotiations.

Focusing on initial commitments to eliminate tariffs and quantitative restrictions, if the pace and pattern of adjustments are not locked into the basic structure of the agreement, the process could easily break down and commitments to liberalize trade could be circumvented--for example a North American version of the Multifiber Agreement could emerge.

Also, it must be recognized that the adjustments to free trade could well be more wrenching in Mexico's traditional manufacturing sector than in the United States and Canada. The temptation to backslide in the United States and Canada could find sympathetic support in Mexico.

In the end, just like phasing schedules for tariffs and quantitative restrictions, the pace of adjustment must be locked into the agreement to ensure that adjustments take place.

FTA Transition Mechanisms and Safeguards

Canada-USA FTA provisions regarding the general elimination of tariffs, quantitative restrictions, horticultural products, and bilateral and global safeguards provide a useful point of departure for considering transition mechanisms and safeguards in trilateral negotiations.

Tariffs

The FTA eliminates tariffs in three groups. Some were cut to zero on January 1, 1989 and all others are being phased out in either five or ten annual increments.[19] Generally, the most vulnerable sectors received the longest transition periods. These included most agricultural and fish products, most wood products, textiles and apparel, footwear, steel, lead, zinc, rail cars, tires, consumer appliances, and precision instruments.[20] The only exception to this ten year deadline is for seasonal tariffs on horticultural products (discussed below).

Various duty drawback and duty remission programs that refund duties on imports that affect bilateral trade will be eliminated by 1998.[21]

19 FTA rules of origin for duty-free treatment require components imported from third countries be incorporated into other goods or be transformed in physically or commercially significant ways. In most cases, this requirement is met when a production process results in a change in tariff classification or 50 percent U.S. and/or Canadian value added. 50 percent content is required for automotive products.

   Apparel made from fabrics imported from third countries will only qualify for duty-free trade up to the following annual limits:

	Non-Woolen	Woolen
	(millions of square yard-equivalent)	
Canadian Exports	50.0	6.0
U.S. Exports	10.5	1.1

20 Overall, of the items subject to duties in the United States and Canada, 15 percent of the tariffs were eliminated immediately, 35 percent were put on five-year phasing and 50 percent were put on ten-year phasing.

21 Duty drawbacks (i.e., refunds of duties on imported goods from third countries that are incorporated into goods and subsequently exported) will not be permitted on Canadian (U.S.) goods destined for the United States (Canada) after January 1994. Products fabricated in Free Trade Zones are not entitled to duty-free treatment when they cross the U.S.-Canadian border. Canadian duty remission programs, outside the automotive sector, which refund tariffs as an incentive to meet domestic performance requirements such as sourcing local products for export or establishing local production facilities, may not be expanded and will be phased out as they expire but no later than January 1998. In the automotive sector, the 13 overseas manufacturers receiving remission of duties on their imports into Canada in exchange for purchasing and exporting components from Canada lost benefits for exports to the United States effective January 1988; all other export-based remission benefits will be phased out by January 1998. Overseas firms receiving duty remission benefits for producing in Canada will lose those benefits when their existing agreements expire but no later than January 1996.

Quantitative Restrictions

Quantitative restrictions on imports are prohibited unless grandfathered or in accordance with GATT rights. This establishes more of a standstill, prohibiting new measures, than it signals new progress.

In the nonagricultural trade, the FTA ended several nuisance restrictions--Canadian embargoes on used aircraft and used automobiles and U.S. embargoes on lottery materials.[22] More importantly, it left in place the gentlemen's agreement concerning Canadian exports of carbon steel to the United States. Although not a formal participant in the U.S. program of VRAs,[23] Canada "monitored" its exports of steel to the United States prior to the FTA, and continues to do so.

In agriculture, the FTA provides for the elimination of Canadian import licensing requirements for oats, wheat and barley when U.S. farm support levels are lowered to Canadian levels. These provisions were intended to protect Canadian farmers from U.S. products receiving higher levels of subsidy and are hard to quarrel with. Canadian import licenses on oats and oat products were lifted in 1989 and on wheat and wheat products in 1991.

The FTA leaves in place quotas that insulate from bilateral competition U.S. producers of sugar and sugar containing products and Canadian producers of poultry and eggs.

Special Provisions for Horticultural Products

All tariffs on fresh fruits and vegetables will be phased out by 1998. However, a special 20 year snapback provision is in place to facilitate adjustment by Canadian growers. They suffer from climatic disadvantages vis-a-vis northern U.S. farmers with parallel growing seasons[24] and have received protection from seasonal tariffs. According to Article 702:

> ...each party reserves the right to apply a temporary duty on fresh fruits or vegetables originating in the territory of the other party and imported into its own territory, when

---

22   Also, it prohibited the reimposition of U.S. restrictions on unprocessed uranium.

23   The United States negotiated VRAs with other major suppliers in October 1984, and these are scheduled to end in March 1992.

24   For example, farmers in Ontario are at disadvantage vis-à-vis growers in the Great Lakes states.

  a) for each of five consecutive working days the import price of
      such fruit or vegetable is below 90 percent of the average
      monthly import price, for the month in which that day falls,
      over the preceding five years, excluding the years with the
      highest and lowest average monthly import price;

  b) the planted acreage in the importing Party for the particular
      fruit or vegetable is no higher than the average acreage over
      the preceding five years, excluding the highest and lowest
      years.[25]

In the first two years of the FTA, the snapback provision was invoked
only once, in April 1990, by Canada for asparagus. This action lasted two
weeks.[26] As discussed in Section III, this mechanism is well designed.
Although it provides protection for a protracted period, this protection is
clearly degressive and fosters adjustment.

Bilateral Safeguard

Regarding safeguards, the FTA establishes rules for both bilateral actions
under the FTA and global actions under GATT Article XIX.

During the transition period, which ends December 31, 1998, either
country may respond to serious injury to domestic producers resulting from
the reduction of duties under the FTA by restoring tariffs for a period of no
longer than three years. Such action may be taken only once in each
industry, and the exporting country is entitled to compensation.[27] The only
exception is the snapback provision for fresh fruits and vegetables.

All disputes regarding safeguard actions are subject to binding
arbitration. Unlike most other disagreements regarding the obligations and
disciplines of the FTA, the consent of both parties is not required for either
party to invoke arbitration.

Global Safeguards

The United States and Canada continue their rights under GATT Article
XIX. However, in taking global actions, they agree to exempt each other

---

25 FTA Article 702, Paragraph 1.a.

26 Office of the United States Trade Representative, *The United States-Canada Free Trade
    Agreement Biennial Report*, Washington, DC: January 1991, p. 13.

27 FTA Article 1101.

except in cases where imports from the other country "are substantial and are contributing importantly to serious injury or threat thereof..."[28] To meet this condition, imports from the United States or Canada must be at least 5 to 10 percent of total imports and an important, though not necessarily the most important, source of injury or threat thereof. If the United States (Canada) determines that imports from Canada (the United States) meet these requirements, Canadian (U.S.) exports to the United States (Canada) may not be reduced "below the trend of imports over a reasonable base period with allowance for growth."[29]

In many industries where the United States is likely to invoke Article XIX or institute a program of VRAs, Canada supplies more than 5 to 10 percent of imports. On the surface, the global track appears to do two things. First, it appears to assure Canada that its industries will no longer be sideswiped in situations in which they are not an important source of injury--this was the case in 1983 when the United States imposed safeguard duties on specialty steel. Second, in the event of a U.S. safeguard action, it gives Canadian producers preferential access to the U.S. market with the opportunity to actually enjoy a limited increase in market shares, as facilitated by the limits placed on third-country market access. This was not the case in the carbon steel program in 1984.[30] This could prove particularly important in many resource-based industries, such as nonferrous metals and minerals.

However, there could be problems. First, formal safeguard actions are increasingly rare and VRAs--such as in steel--are the norm. Richardson warns, because FTA Article 1102 does not explicitly mention VRAs, U.S.

---

28 FTA Article 1102, Paragraph 1.

29 FTA Article 1102, Paragraph 4b.

30 In parallel to its formal program of VRAs, the United States jawboned Canadian producers to keep their shipments at less than 4 percent of U.S. consumption prior to the FTA. In 1986, 1987 and 1988 (the three years prior to the FTA), the Canadian shares of the U.S. market were 3.9 percent, 3.9 percent and 3.4 percent, respectively. In 1989 and 1990, they were 3.3 and 3.2 percent. U.S. International Trade Commission, *Quarterly Report on the Status of the Steel Industry*, USITC Publication 2336, Washington, DC: December 1990, Tables 6 and 7; *Monthly Report on the Status of the Steel Industry*, USITC Publication 2130, Washington, DC: October 1988, Table 8.

officials could argue that Article 1102 does not apply.[31] Even within the context of a straightforward GATT Article XIX action, defining a limit on Canadian exports consistent with "the trend of imports over a reasonable base period with allowance for growth" will prove difficult. In Richardson's words, invoking this provision "is tantamount to a selective VRA."[32] Within the context of a straightforward safeguard action, applying this language:

> virtually invites the kinds of grudging negotiation (What base period is "reasonable"? Do "growth" rates have to be positive numbers?) that frequently give birth to any VRA.[33]

This provision of the FTA is yet to be tested. Another politically hot adjustment problem involving Canadian exporters, such as could occur in nonferrous metals, could precipitate a crisis for the FTA. This issue needs to be clarified and, if necessary, addressed before an unmanageable problem surfaces. Trilateral negotiations may provide such an opportunity.

Second, the market sharing arrangement envisioned by FTA Article 1102 would impose costs on other trading partners, who would likely face greater reductions in their exports when the United States takes formal safeguard actions or seeks VRAs. In steel, Canada's market share was growing prior to the FTA and its sales accounted for about a fifth of U.S. imports. Permitting Canada's market share to increase would have substantially exacerbated the reductions in sales imposed on other U.S. suppliers. In a bilateral or trilateral arrangement with Mexico, it would be reasonable for Mexico to expect considerations from the United States comparable to those afforded Canada, and this would aggravate this crowding out problem.

Structuring Transition Mechanisms and Safeguards for a Trilateral Agreement

The findings of the careful quantitative studies notwithstanding, the transition mechanisms and safeguards in an agreement with Mexico must be

31 Richardson, J. David, "Adjustments and Safeguards," in Peter Morici, ed., *Making Free Trade Work: The Canada-U.S. Agreement*, New York: Council on Foreign Relations, 1990, pp. 68-70.

32 *Ibid.* p. 69.

33 *Ibid.*

fashioned to accommodate adjustments more severe than those anticipated from the Canada-USA FTA.

I argue that there are reasons to expect this to be the case. These include the direct consequences of free trade on: the pace of economic reform in Mexico; incentives for the managers of Maquiladoras; and the expectations of offshore investors and expatriate Mexican capital. They also include: the indirect effects of free trade on other adjustment dynamics already at work in the U.S. economy.

Whether or not these predictions prove out, as discussed immediately below, the climate in Washington requires that the transition mechanisms and safeguards be fashioned to meet these eventualities. Clearly, the trick is to fashion mechanisms that prepare us for the worst and respond to the political pressures acting on Washington, Ottawa and Mexico City *but* do so in a manner that does not impede adjustment if the economic models are correct and labour dislocations are small and not widespread.

Political Environment

During the Congressional debate concerning approval of fast track negotiating authority from March to May 1991, concerns about labour market dislocations surfaced as a major issue. For example, House Majority Leader Richard Gephart, in his letter of March 27 to President Bush, stated:

> for a free-trade agreement to be a meaningful benefit to both nations, it must contain provisions that will stem any hemorrhage of American jobs across the border.[34]

Expressing scepticism about the findings of recent studies regarding the scope of potential adjustments and noting the particular problems posed by large wage disparities between the United States and Mexico he stated:

> We recognize that the U.S.-Canada FTA will be phased in over a ten year period. It is possible that we may need to allow for as long, if not a longer phase-in period in the case of Mexico. We may want to examine the possibility of phasing in the provisions of a final agreement based on increasing standards of living in Mexico. This will provide the Mexican government with the incentive to continue with their liberalization program as well as

---

34 Letter from House Majority Leader Richard A. Gephart to President George Bush, March 27, 1991.

providing U.S. workers with a greater protection against a competitive policy based on wage differentials alone.[35]

Regarding safeguards he stated:

> ...it is important that a comprehensive escape clause provision ... can act as stop gap measure to stem the loss of jobs and business opportunities if there is a hemorrhaging in any one sector. This provision should have a trigger that will allow us to ameliorate any negative impact on a sector and reassess what course of action to take.[36]

So intense was the pressure from Congress, President Bush, in his reply to Representative Gephart and a joint letter from Senate Finance Chairman Lloyd Bentsen and House Ways and Means Chairman Dan Rostenkowski, stated:

> To avoid dislocations to industries and workers producing goods that are import-sensitive, tariff and *nontariff barriers* on such products should be eliminated in small increments over a time period sufficient to ensure orderly adjustment.
>
> We will be prepared to consider transition periods beyond those in the U.S.-Canada FTA.[37]

With regard to safeguards:

> Even where tariffs and other barriers are staged over a lengthy period, there may be isolated cases in which injurious increases in imports could occur. To prevent injury from such increases, we will seek to include in the agreement a procedure allowing temporary reimposition of duties and other restrictions.

---

35   *Ibid.*

36   In addition, Representative Gephart noted the importance of ensuring adequate workplace health and safety standards in Mexico, and he stated with regard to lax Mexican environmental enforcement:

> ...it is tough for U.S. companies to compete against firms that operate under a more lax environment. This laxity can, in fact, operate as a subsidy.

Economists can debate whether this an adequate assessment but once Congress concludes something is a subsidy, it is hard to undo the consequences of that thinking for the conduct of trade policy. Sceptics should consider the trials of the Canadian softwood lumber industry.

37   President of the United States [George Bush], *Response of the Administration to Issues Raised in Connection with the Negotiation of A North American Free Trade Agreement: Executive Summary*, Washington, May 1, 1991, p. 1--emphasis added.

This mechanism should be designed to respond quickly, especially in cases of sudden import increases.

Special "snap-back" provisions should be included to address the unique problems faced by producers of perishable products.[38]

Essentially, it appears that the President has promised to phase-out quotas and other nontariff barriers and to seek a snapback provision for horticultural products similar to those in the FTA.

Pressure on these issues continued through the summer of 1991, and in August 1991, the President acknowledged before the National Governors Association:

If we bring back a trade agreement ... not considerate of the disparity of wages (between the United States and Mexico) ... the agreement won't pass.[39]

Effective Transition Mechanisms

To be effective, transition mechanisms and safeguards must meet five, sometimes competing, sets of competing objectives:

First, schedules for the phased elimination of tariffs and the effects of quotas schedules should anticipate a time path of resource reallocation that maximizes the balance between the long-term gains from the redeployment of labour and capital and the short-term costs of underemployment of some of these resources. The latter will vary among specific industries and will depend on the capacity of labour markets, firms and workers to acclimatize to more intense competition and the effects of adjustment assistance programs on this capacity.

In this regard, some industries now subject to quantitative restrictions may require special consideration.[40] For the United States, apparel and steel (if voluntary restraints agreements are extended beyond 1992) may

---

38   *Ibid.* p. 2.

39   Maggs, John, "Environment, US-Canada Issues Dominate Debut of Trade Talks," *Journal of Commerce*, August 20, 1991, p. 10A.

40   In the Canada-U.S. FTA, the important problem areas were not addressed--U.S. restrictions on imports of sugar and sugar containing products and Canadian restrictions on imports of poultry and eggs remain impediments to bilateral trade, as does the gentlemen's agreement limiting Canadian steel shipments to the United States.

require special handling.[41] In Mexico, limits on imports of automobiles, which are being relaxed but not eliminated may require special treatment.[42]

Also, an analog to the FTA provisions for horticultural products may be necessary to ease adjustments for southern U.S. fruit and vegetable producers.

Second, it is essential to craft safeguard provisions that offer credible relief, quickly, before situations get out of hand, and do so in ways that do not derail the adjustment processes, disrupt the continued processes of lowering tariffs and removing other trade barriers or permit political pressures to build for remedies outside the trade agreement--e.g., continental VRAs. To this end, safeguard protection must be credibly temporary and degressive. It must provide enough breathing space and without the prospect of a permanent halt in the growth of import market shares (absent a fundamental improvement in the cost competitiveness of domestic producers).

Third, transition mechanisms and safeguards must acknowledge the political environment in which Members of Congress and Parliament operate. In a more outward-looking Mexican economy, continued economic reform, coupled with low-wages and renewed confidence among U.S., Japanese and EC investors, may do as much or more to create import competition for U.S. producers than the elimination of tariff and quantitative restrictions. Given the apparent inability of politicians and their constituents to discern causality when confronted with intense import competition, it is essential that the phased elimination of tariffs and quotas acknowledge the importance of wage differentials in some sectors by affording long periods for adjustment and by linking access to resort to safeguard protection to implementation of sector-specific adjustment assistance efforts. These may prove to be the most effective ways to head off special pleading and backsliding on commitments to phase out tariffs and quantitative

---

41 Canada does not currently limit imports of Mexican steel and apparel but a special regime for the U.S. imports in a trilateral agreement could necessitate similar provisions for Canadian imports.

42 In 1991, the value of exports must exceed the value of imports by a ratio of 2.5 to 1. This requirement falls to 1.75 to 1 in 1991.

restrictions, abuse of safeguard mechanisms and resort to North American Free Trade Agreement analogues of extra-GATT mechanisms.[43]

Fourth, transition mechanisms should not provide any specific benefits, considerations or remedies--such as those envisioned because of Mexican wage advantages--to industries where, as many economists expect, adjustments are small. Whatever mechanisms are constructed to accommodate lower Mexican wages, they should be inoperative if the tariff phasing is enough to facilitate orderly adjustment.

Fifth, transition mechanisms should have an automatic sunset.

Tariffs and Quantitative Restrictions

The problem of tariffs is fairly straightforward. Given sentiments in Congress, comparable political sensitivities in Canada and the scope of adjustment expected for Mexico, the FTA notion of three tariff groups-- immediate elimination, five-year phasing and ten-year phasing--may have to be augmented to include a fourth group slated for 15- or 20-year phasing. It should be noted, 20-year phasing would only have meaning for tariffs higher than 20 percent, such as trucks and some apparel items in the United States. Although tariff spikes tend to be in the more import-sensitive industries and 20-year planning could prove an asset in selling the agreement to sceptics in the Congress and Parliament resort to a phase-in period of this length should be as limited as possible.

Generally, quantitative restrictions, including those imposed by investment performance requirements,[44] should be converted to tariffs (tariffication), and these "equivalent tariffs" should be phased out with MFN tariffs. As noted above, the United States will require special provisions to phase out apparel, and perhaps steel, quotas.

Horticultural Products

As in the U.S.-Canadian agreement, horticultural products are a sensitive area. This time around, it is U.S. growers that are at a climatic

---

43 In addition, although not a transition or safeguard issue in the sense of this paper, efforts to assist Mexico in improving its workplace health and safety and environmental enforcement would be useful in dissipating incentives to backslide.

44 For example, Mexico's practice of linking automotive imports to exports--see footnote 41.

disadvantage vis-à-vis Mexican farmers in products such as tomatoes, cucumbers, bell peppers, broccoli, onions, and strawberries.[45] Applying the FTA provisions or some iteration to U.S. tariffs on fresh fruits and vegetables makes considerable sense. Although this provision offers the option of temporary protection for a protracted period, it contains a strong bias towards adjustment. First, price floors are expressed in nominal terms; therefore, inflation should lower the real value of these price guarantees to farmers, gradually, over a 20-year period. Yet, the necessity to become more efficient or reallocate resources is inevitable. Even a modest 4 percent rate of inflation would halve the real value of price floors in less than 12 years.

Second, the 5-year moving average method for setting the price trigger for seasonal tariffs will permit a gradual decline in the nominal floor price, should free trade lead to a secular decline in market prices for Canadian fruits and vegetables during the harvest season. This should guarantee enough revenue for incumbent farmers to retire debt. To the extent a secular decline in crop prices reduces real land values, these reduced values are phased in gently--20 years is an adequate period to amortize a gradual decline in crop values.

Third, the FTA snapback provision requires that the land under cultivation (grapes are an exception) remain constant or decline for snapback tariffs to be invoked.

Bilateral Safeguard Provisions

As in the Canada-USA FTA, provisions for bilateral and global safeguard action will be necessary in an agreement with Mexico.

As discussed above, the FTA bilateral safeguards are limited to the ten-year period of phased tariff reductions and may be invoked only once by an industry. Given the wage and productivity disparities between the United States and Mexico, it may be necessary to offer more generous terms, if national governments are not to be tempted to go around safeguard provisions by seeking VRAs or resorting to the creative use of trade remedy laws.

---

45 In crafting a mechanism, it is important to recognize that growing seasons in Canada do not coincide with growing seasons in California, Texas and Mexico; therefore, Canada does not apply seasonal tariffs at the same time as the United States. It would not serve Canada's interest for a snapback provision raising prices in the U.S. market to affect prices in the Canadian market.

In this regard, the FTA mechanism could be adopted with two innovations. First, bilateral safeguards should be made available for a period of 15 years for products slotted for 20-year tariff-phase; this safeguard window could be extended to 20 years as well. Second, as in the FTA, each bilateral safeguard action should be limited to three years and each industry should receive such relief only once without any strings attached. However, each country in seeking such relief for an industry for the first time should be required to demonstrate a credible adjustment program for retraining and redeploying workers in the most distressed segments of the industry *or* forfeit the right to apply for safeguard tariffs for that industry again in the future. Also, a minimum three-year waiting period, should be imposed between safeguard actions.

Adjustment efforts could be certified by an independent binational or trinational arbitration panel at the beginning of each year throughout the safeguard period. Failure by a national government to appropriate the funds deemed necessary by the arbitration panel would result in suspension of the safeguard action.

Global Safeguards

With regard to global safeguard actions that the United States, Canada or Mexico might take under GATT Article XIX, it seems reasonable to trilateralize the provisions of the FTA. In many products in which the United States, Canada or Mexico are likely to take safeguard actions, or extra-GATT remedies having similar purposes, at least one of its three continental trading partners would likely be found to be a "substantial source of injury" (i.e., supplied more than 5 or 10 percent of imports), and affected partners would expect that their exports would not be reduced below their trend over "a reasonable base period with allowance for growth." However, as discussed in Section II, this language is vague and could pose problems down the road.[46] Trilateral negotiations provide a good opportunity to tighten up these provisions.

Also, the market sharing arrangement envisioned by Article 1102 would impose considerable costs on other U.S. trading partners if the United States was compelled to give both Canada and Mexico preferential and growing

---

46 See David Richardson, (1990) and Morici, Peter, *A New Special Relationship: Free Trade and Canada-U.S. Relations in the 1990s*, Ottawa: Institute for Research on Public Policy, in press.

access to its market under any future global safeguard action or program of VRAs.

Special Provisions for Apparel

As noted above the U.S. apparel sector may present special problems.[47] As in many industries, the apparel sector was encouraged to be domestically oriented by Mexico's import-substitution strategy during from the 1940s through the 1970s. As a consequence, its share of the U.S. market, and its allocations of U.S. Multifiber Agreement imports were small prior to the late 1980s.

In the U.S. apparel sector, import penetration ranges between 30 and 40 percent, and Mexico accounts for only about 5 percent of U.S. imports. In 1988, the United States and Mexico negotiated a bilateral agreement that raised Mexico's quotas--this should permit overall Mexican textile and apparel exports to the United States to increase about 6 percent a year through 1991.[48] This agreement established the so-called Special Regime requiring the use of U.S. materials in many of Mexico's apparel exports.[49]

Free trade could cause a large and rapid movement of apparel production from the United States to Mexico. It is imperative that the negotiators craft mechanisms that promote, indeed require, the redeployment of capital and labour but do so at a pace that does not cause in the words Congressman Gephart a "hemorrhage of American jobs" lest the Congress demand measures that steps be taken to "ameliorate any negative impact on a sector" and cause us to "reassess what course of action to take." Such a reassessment would be a recipe for backsliding on basic commitments to liberalize trade, creating North American versions of the

---

47 Should the steel VRA continue past March 1992, a mechanism for basic steel similar to the one proposed here for apparel could be required as much for political as economic reasons.

48 These quotas were further liberalized in 1990.

49 A portion of each quota is reserved for Special Regime goods, which are among the products made in Maquiladora plants. These exports, which comprise 50 to 90 percent of various categories of Mexican apparel exports to the United States, must be assembled from U.S.-fabricated components, and the fabric must be wholly formed and cut in the United States. See International Trade Commission, *Review of Trade and Investment Liberalization Measures by Mexico and Prospects for Future United States-Mexican Relations*, Report No. 2275, April 1990, pp. 2-5.

Multifiber Agreement, and the undermining of the fundamental integrity of the free trade agreement.

Merely converting existing quotas to equivalent tariffs to reflect this reality could create numerous distortions. For one thing, equivalent tariffs for some products would be much higher than MFN rates and make affected Mexican apparel much more expensive than products from other countries;[50] this would depress Mexican wages and discourage modernization in that sector.

As the Maquiladora experience indicates, the U.S. and Mexican textile and apparel sectors offer substantial opportunities for complementary production and the above mentioned price distortions created by simple tariffication would discourage this process. Whatever mechanism is put in place for apparel, it should encourage and not discourage the development of a more integrated and competitive North American industry.

Several alternatives to simple tariffication are available. First, don't convert the apparel quotas into tariff equivalents; instead phase out the MFN tariffs over 20 years and aggressively increase Mexico's quotas each year. For example, Mexico's share of U.S. consumption of apparel overall could be permitted to rise "G" percentage points a year or by some agreed upon schedule enumerated in the agreement.[51] Currently, Mexico exports to the United States equal about 2 percent of U.S. consumption. Mexico's quotas under the Multifiber Agreement could be increased each year by amounts equal to 1 or 2 percentage points of U.S. consumption. Essentially, this would entail an extension of the 1988 agreement noted above but with much more liberal terms--namely, a much higher growth rate for Mexican exports.[52] This provision could be structured so as to sunset within 20 years by setting G high enough to make quotas no longer relevant within

---

50   During the early years of a trade agreement, Mexican apparel entering the United States would be subject to a higher tariff than the MFN rate on apparel from other foreign countries, including those entering from Caribbean countries.

51   It is important that a growth rate(s) or schedule be included in the text of the agreement so that the U.S. industry knows how quickly it will have to adjust and to lock in the adjustment process.

52   See footnote 48.

that period and by requiring elimination of all quotas at the end of that period.[53]

A second more liberal approach would be to suspend, immediately, duties on imports currently entering the United States from Mexico under existing quotas and each year increase Mexican imports entering the United States duty free by an amount equal to "G" percent of U.S. consumption--again, perhaps by one or two percentage points. Imports above this level could enter at the MFN duty plus the equivalent tariff of existing quotas; this higher tariff would be subject to phased elimination over a 20-year period.

Further, in computing permitted Mexican duty-free imports, credit could be given for increased U.S. sales of apparel and textiles in Mexico so that increased U.S. exports and intraindustry specialization would partially compensate for the growth of Mexican sales in the United States.

For example, suppose in the shirt industry U.S. imports and exports with Mexico were M(b) and X(b) percent of U.S. apparent consumption[54] in the base year prior to the agreement; M(b-1) and X(b-1) are similarly defined for the year prior to the base year. In year one of the agreement, duty-free U.S. imports from Mexico as a share of U.S. consumption would be limited to:

$$M(1) = M(b) + G + [X(b) - X(b-1)] \tag{1}$$

In year n, duty free imports would be limited to:

$$M(n) = M(b) + n(G) + [X(n-1) - X(b-1)] \tag{2}$$

Imports above $M(n)$ would not be excluded but would pay the following tariff:

$$T = \{T_{mfn} + T_q] / [20 - n / 20]$$

Where T_{mfn} is the GATT-bound, MFN tariff at the beginning of the agreement and T_q is the additional protection afforded by quotas. Values for

---

53 As in the alternative suggested immediately below, different values of G could be specified for various subsectors of the industry. However, for each subsector, the value of G would have to be set high enough to ensure that the effects of quotas abate within the 20-year transition period.

54 Apparent consumption is equal to shipments plus imports less exports.

G and T_q would be established in negotiations and designated in the text of the Free Trade Agreement.

This mechanism would have several virtues.

- By immediately eliminating duties on existing Mexican exports and opening the U.S. market to additional Mexican exports at tariffs equivalent to the combined protection provided by MFN tariffs and existing quotas, this mechanism would immediately liberalize trade. Also, by eliminating tariffs on existing imports, this mechanism would end U.S. sourcing requirements imposed by the Special Regime and replace the latter with more general incentives for Mexico to source fabric, components and finished garments in the United States. These general incentives would impose fewer distortions on resource allocation decisions than the Special Regime.

- By permitting a different G for each subsector named in the free-trade agreement, this mechanism would accommodate varying capacities to cope with import competition and adjustment among various U.S. subsectors and in particular communities.

- This mechanism would both establish a market-normed annual growth of duty-free Mexican exports that U.S. domestic producers would have to accept *and* specify in advance the remedy afforded to domestic producers should that rate of growth be exceeded. This remedy would be limited to the tariff-equivalent protection received by the industry prior to the agreement, and such tariffs would only be applied to incremental Mexican exports.

- By freezing G prior to initiating the free trade agreement, this mechanism would
  - •• limit but lock-in expected rates of adjustment for U.S. domestic producers in import-sensitive industries;
  - •• provide credible relief, quickly, before situations got out of hand, and do so in way that did not derail adjustment, disrupt the continued process of removing trade barriers, or permit political pressures to build for remedies outside the free trade agreement--e.g., continental VRAs;
  - •• provide credibly temporary and degressive protection because, n(G) and M(n)--i.e., the share of domestic sales that could enter duty free--would be larger each year.

- If the annual increase in Mexican exports net of Mexican imports does not exceed G percent of U.S. consumption (and hence labour market adjustments are small), this mechanism becomes inoperative.

- Since n(G) must reach 100 by the year 100/n(G), the mechanism has an automatic sunset.

In return for accepting such a mechanism for apparel, Mexico would expect concessions on other issues--perhaps it would seek phased elimination of its export performance requirements for autos or phased elimination of some of its other import licenses.

Conclusions

A free trade agreement with Mexico offers the United States and Canada important opportunities to increase continental specialization and improve their industrial competitiveness vis-a-vis Japan and the EC. However, to assure these gains are realized, adjustment should be paced by transition mechanisms that recognize the capacities of firms and workers in individual industries to relocate and retrain. In the event adjustment pressures are greater than anticipated, safeguards should offer credibly temporarily and degressive relief.

Transition mechanisms should recognize the pressures faced by politicians in Washington and elsewhere to gradually phase out both tariffs and nontariff barriers and to respond to the competitive consequences of low Mexican wages. Safeguards are needed that offer relief quickly, before situations get out of hand, and do so in ways that do not derail the adjustment process or permit political pressures to build for remedies outside the disciplines of the free trade agreement, such as VRAs.

To this end, tariffs should be phased out in periods up to 20 years. Generally, quantitative restrictions should be converted to tariffs, and these tariffs should be phased out along with MFN tariffs. As a safeguard it should be possible to reinstate tariffs for three years, in a manner similar to the bilateral safeguard provisions of the USA-Canada FTA. Additionally, such relief should be made available for a period up to 20 years. Also, governments should be permitted to invoke safeguards more than once in each industry, if they put in place aggressive programs to retrain and redeploy workers each time they seek safeguard protection for an industry. If a government failed to follow through on such a commitment, the safeguard action would be suspended. Binational/trinational arbitration panels should review safeguard actions (such arbitration may be invoked by either party in the Canada-USA FTA) and certify the progress of adjustment assistance programs.

For horticultural fruits and vegetables, a snapback provision to cushion adjustment for U.S. farmers, similar to the one in place for Canadian growers under the FTA, seems appropriate.

Finally, a mechanism should be crafted that phases out quotas in the apparel sector. The one suggested here would permit Mexican exports to grow much more rapidly than they have historically and eliminate those provisions of the Special Regime that require the use of U.S. fabric and components. In place of the latter, other incentives, which would impose fewer distortions on resource allocation decisions, would be put in place to encourage the purchase of U.S. fabric, components and finished garments.

Chapter 5

Subsidy and Countervailing Duty Issues in the Context of North American Economic Integration

Sven W. Arndt, William H. Kaempfer and Thomas D. Willett

Introduction

The role of subsidies in international trade is a hotly contested issue, whose resolution has escaped concerted efforts at multilateral as well as bilateral levels. Although the Tokyo Round trade negotiations made some headway in dealing with the problem, they failed to resolve it. Efforts to establish acceptable subsidy codes at regional and bilateral levels have not fared much better. The issue was a key component, for example, of the Canada-USA free trade negotiations, but there, too, resolution was not attainable. The problem arises partly from different perceptions of the role of the state in the promotion of economic activity. Europeans tend to be more interventionist, for example, than Americans, although Americans see themselves as less interventionist than they really are. Developing countries, for their part, justify intervention on infant-industry grounds and remind the USA and other advanced nations of the importance of such policies in their own industrial histories.

Indeed, one of the difficulties in dealing with subsidies is to define and then distinguish between "good" and "bad" subsidies. A subsidy which would, in a perfect world, be labelled prejudicial, may in a world of imperfect markets and imperfect policies merely serve to offset existing distortions. Defining and identifying beneficial subsidies and separating them from their distorting and anti-competitive counterparts is, however, a very difficult task.

Common logic suggests that subsidies which have no effect on other countries do not warrant intervention on the part of the international community, no matter how distorting they are. The reason is that the cost of such distortions falls entirely on the subsidizing country. Under U.S. law, however, the executive branch is obliged to retaliate against subsidies of this type. This paradox may be explained in part by the fact that policymakers in the USA do not always fully understand the problem they are supposed to solve and do not always carefully weigh the interests they are serving in seeking solutions to the problem. Not infrequently, the interests of particular producers are treated as if they were identical with those of the nation.

One of the major disagreements between the United States and other countries pertains to the role of subsidies in economic policy. Americans believe that their country's markets are relatively free of government intervention. Europeans and others assert that the difference is mainly one of style and that much of U.S. support to industry is hidden in the defense budget and behind national security arguments.

Be that as it may, the primary U.S. goal in international negotiations at various levels has been to force other countries to relinquish subsidies as a policy tool. The negotiating objective of America's trading partners, on the other hand, has been to curb U.S. anti-subsidy policies. These differences in objectives have contributed to repeated stalemates at the negotiating table.

One point of contention has been to define and identify national subsidies that are harmful to the interests of other countries and to separate them from those that are not. Another has been to design constructive countermeasures to harmful subsidies. U.S. policy has been very unclear on both fronts. At times the primary U.S. goal has appeared to be one of merely "leveling the playing field," in which case a countervailing duty should be just large enough to offset the adverse effects of foreign subsidies. At other times, the principal thrust of U.S. policy has appeared to be punitive, that is, to punish trading partners for using subsidies, regardless of their external effects. At still other times, the objective appears to have been preservation of the competitive advantage of particular U.S. industries.

When the United States and Canada began their trade talks, the hope was widespread that new ground would be broken on the issue of subsidies and that the bilateral agreement would serve as a guide and example for Uruguay Round negotiators. Those hopes were not realized, as the problem turned out to be no more amenable to resolution between two close and largely similar neighbours, than in the context of multilateral talks. In the

Canada-USA agreement, the subsidies issue was ultimately reserved for follow-up negotiations which to date have made little progress. With the prospective addition of Mexico in a North American Free Trade Area, the importance of dealing with these issues takes on additional urgency.

The issue is extraordinarily complex, analytically, empirically, and in relation to the formulation and implementation of policy. The discussion that follows addresses some, but by no means all, of the salient issues in the context of the North-American free trade negotiations. There is no reason to suppose that the trilateral negotiations now in progress will be more successful in resolving the issue of subsidies and their antidotes than the GATT and the USA-Canada bilateral.

The next section provides an overview of the salient issues. The paper then considers some general effects of domestic subsidies on a country's trading partners. The penultimate section examines alternative strategies of response to foreign subsidies. It is followed by concluding comments.

An Overview of CVD-Subsidy Issues

The United States has been by far the most frequent user of CVDs. As a result of various grandfathering provisions in U.S. trade legislation and recognized by the GATT, the U. S. has not been bound by requirements that restrict CVDs to cases of material injury.

Countervailing duty investigations begin with petitions to the Commerce Department and International Trade Commission (ITC) by a domestic party alleging that goods entering the U.S. market from abroad are the beneficiaries of foreign subsidies.[1] The responsibility of the Commerce Department is to determine if the imports in question are in fact benefitting from a subsidy, while the ITC tends to focus on issues of injury. If both Commerce and the ITC make an initial positive ruling, the importer in question must post bond guaranteeing payment of the CVD if the ruling is upheld.[2] This bonding procedure, or "suspension of liquidation," is important in that it brings the exporting firm directly into the investigation.

Once the initial rulings are issued, there follows a period of up to four months of suspension of liquidation before the final determination is issued.

---

1   Finger, J. Michael, and Tracy Murray, "Policing Unfair Imports: The United States Example," *Journal of World Trade*, Vol. 24, No. 4, August 1990, provide a detailed description of the entire CVD procedure in the USA.

2   Even if the initial ruling by Commerce is negative, the investigation continues, but no bond need be posted. See Finger and Murray (1990), p. 40.

The importer and the injured domestic industry may at any time during this period reach a negotiated settlement which either eliminates the subsidy or limits the extent of market disruption by means of a voluntary export restraint or a price undertaking.[3] Negotiated settlements void producer petitions and thereby close the case. In the absence of negotiated settlements, a final ruling of subsidy and injury is required and, if positive, is followed by imposition of a countervailing duty.

Current CVD policies and procedures create strong incentives for "out-of-court" settlements and thereby encourage collusion and legitimize cartelization. The domestic firm has an incentive to reach a collusive agreement, because it cannot be sure that the initial positive ruling on subsidization with injury will not be reversed in the final stage. In the presence of this type of uncertainty, price undertakings or VERs represent an attractive alternative to the risk-averse domestic petitioner.

Although a negotiated settlement eliminates any possibility of a negative final ruling of subsidy or injury, it nevertheless offers advantages to the foreign exporter, particularly if it spawns VERs that facilitate cartelization of relevant markets. It brings immediate lifting of the suspension of liquidation and thereby eliminates the disruptive effects of prolonged uncertainty. There is, of course, less incentive for the exporter to negotiate a settlement to eliminate the subsidy if it does not leave room for cartelization. Such an agreement not only eliminates the benefit of subsidized production destined for the U.S. market, but may erode political support at home for production subsidies of exports aimed at third markets.

Development of a new international code on subsidies was one of the major issues on the agenda of the Tokyo Round of trade negotiations in the late 1970s. Although a code was negotiated, it fell far short of most expectations,[4] in part because fundamental differences among countries precluded a strong and comprehensive agreement. The negotiations broke

---

3   A price undertaking is an agreement to establish a minimum price floor for exports to the domestic market. As Hufbauer notes, "the worst punishment coming out of a CVD proceeding is that the offender is told to raise his prices--hardly an effective deterrent." Hufbauer, C. Gary, "Subsidies," in Jeffrey J. Schott, ed., *Completing the Uruguay Round*, Washington, DC: Institute for International Economics, September 1990, p. 106.

4   See, for example, Stern, R., and B. Hochman, "The Codes Approach," in J. Michael Finger, and A. Olechowski, eds., *The Uruguay Round: A Handbook for the Multilateral Trade Negotiations*, Washington, DC: The World Bank, 1987; and Tarullo, D.K., "The MTN Subsidies Code: Agreement Without Consensus," in S.J. Rubin, and G.C. Hufbauer, eds., *Emerging Standards of International Trade and Investment*, Totowa, IA: Rowman and Allanheld, 1983.

little new ground on the central question of the definition of subsidies requiring international surveillance and control. The hope, moreover, that the gradual development of case law would provide practical answers to this question has so far not been realized.

The experience of the Tokyo Round negotiations on a subsidies code demonstrates the magnitude of the philosophical gaps that separate countries on this issue. While many governments openly espouse and pursue interventionist industrial policies and developmental strategies, the official United States position, not always reflected in practice and policy, is opposed to intervention.

Subsidies and the USA-Canada Bilateral

The bilateral negotiations on the free trade area between the United States and Canada addressed the issue, but failed to reach a resolution, in spite of hopes on both sides that establishment of a comprehensive code might serve as a model for the Uruguay Round. Although Canada did succeed in placing some restraints on U.S. process protectionism, fundamental disagreements in a number of areas of principle kept the two nations from reaching a comprehensive agreement. In the matter of process, the USA agreed to prior consultation on prospective changes in countervailing duty law and to binding arbitration in bilateral CVD disputes, but little headway was made on the issue of subsidy discipline itself.[5] This issue is likely to be at the core of the upcoming negotiations with Mexico, where it will be no more amenable to resolution than before, unless the negotiating parties can reconcile some of their philosophical differences. The USA, for its part, will have to clarify the objectives of policy in this respect. Many past CVD actions have done more, others less, than achieve a "level playing field." Policy has encouraged rather than rectified inefficient resource utilization; it has contributed to the cartelization of markets; and it has, by allowing VER settlements, strengthened the long-run competitiveness of foreign producers.

Among the unresolved and outstanding problems between the USA and Canada are agricultural subsidies, which are important to both countries; the treatment of subsidies at sub-federal levels; and the general role of domestic subsidies, given Canada's historical reliance on intervention of this type.

---

5   See Schott, Jeffrey J., and Murray G. Smith, eds., *The Canada-United States Free Trade Agreement: The Global Impact*, Washington, DC: Washington Institute for International Economics, 1988, p. 44.

Fears that curtailment of subsidy policies would weaken competitiveness in relation to third countries added to Canada's reluctance to fashion a comprehensive, albeit bilateral, accord. In the end, the two countries agreed to disagree and to attempt to resolve their disagreements in ongoing negotiations within the bilateral Working Group on Subsidies.

Substantive Issues in the Treatment of Subsidies

From the standpoint of traditional national economic efficiency considerations, concerns about foreign subsidies make little sense. Foreign restrictions on international trade have been a legitimate area of concern because of their adverse effects on the importing country's terms of trade. Foreign subsidies, on the other hand, improve the importing country's terms of trade. While such subsidies may not be in the aggregate economic interests of the country granting them, trade theory suggests that the importing country should take full advantage of the reduced cost of imports.

An important exception, long recognized in the literature on anti-dumping, is the possibility that predatory subsidies could be used to drive competitors out of business, leaving the market ripe for subsequent monopoly pricing. The conditions necessary for successful predation are quite stringent, however, so that the need for international concern over this possibility is likely to be quite limited.[6] More recently, analytical work in the context of strategic trade theory has shown that foreign subsidies could under certain oligopolistic market structures generate net losses for the importing country. Here too, however, research suggests that the policy relevance of such concerns is quite limited.[7] Furthermore, in both the predatory pricing and strategic trade policy cases, the most effective response by the importing country tends to be case-specific rather than a broad policy regime of countervailing duties against all subsidies.

Market intervention through subsidies has been justified in a variety of ways, many of which cannot sustain close analytical scrutiny. Production and export subsidies are economically justifiable if their purpose is to

---

6   See Yeager, Leland B., and David G. Tuerck, *Trade Policy and the Price System*, Scranton, PA: International, 1966 and Jackson, J.H., "Perspectives on Countervailing Duties," *Law and Policy in International Business*, Vol. 21, No. 4, 1990.

7   See, for example, Baldwin, Robert T., "Strategic Trade Policy," JEL (forthcoming); and Haberler, Gottfried, "Strategic Trade Policy and the New International Economics: A Critical Analysis," in R.W. Jones, and A.O. Krueger, eds., *The Political Economy of International Trade*, Cambridge, MA: Basil-Blackwell, 1989.

counteract market imperfections and distortions. A widely recognized category of "imperfections" justifying intervention arises in the context of externalities that will not or cannot be internalized by private agents. In these and similar cases, subsidies are an economically efficient--albeit fiscally costly--form of intervention to minimize the "deadweight" costs of distortions. Subsidies of this type belong to the class of so-called benign subsidies and are not countervailable in principle.

However, it is often not easy in practice to distinguish between benign and distorting subsidies and, in case of either, to determine the precise nature of the distortions. Subsidies are easily and frequently abused. Rent-seeking through the political system by well-organized interest groups can lead to subsidies which neither offset distortions nor create beneficial externalities.

Hufbauer (1990) has suggested that subsidies were probably overused prior to the late 1980s, but that their use and their impact on international trade have recently declined in many countries. Reasons given by Hufbauer include budget constraints brought on by competition from other interest groups (e.g. health, education, the elderly, and environmental interests), growing public scepticism about the costs and benefits of industrial policies, and the international debt crisis.

Even where justification for countervailing duties can be shown to exist in principle, determining the size of the duty is fraught with difficulties. It is rarely the case that the optimal size of the duty matches the size of the nominal subsidy. The former is very typically smaller than the latter, and may in some non-trivial cases be negative.[8] Determining the correct size of a countervailing duty becomes especially troublesome in the context of subsidies, in which the distorting, and hence countervailable, effects of various subsidies may be interdependent, but offsetting in some instances and reinforcing in others. In such an environment, countervailing duties may not only increase the overall degree of distortions in world markets, but worsen the competitive position of the very domestic producers they are designed to protect.

In most cases of countervailing duties, the required size of the duty is a function of the stated objective; it will vary depending on whether that objective is to level the playing field, punish the subsidizing country, or collect revenue. There is scant evidence that U.S. policymakers are clear

---

8   See Gaisford, D. James, and Donald L. McLachlan, "Domestic Subsidies and Countervail: The Treacherous Ground of the Level Playing Field," *Journal of World Trade*, Vol. 24, No. 4, August 1990.

on these issues, in spite of the official rhetoric stressing the level-playing-field objective.[9]

Conflicting Policy Objectives

Not only do U.S. policy objectives on this issue appear muddled and driven by interest-group pressures and preferences rather than clearly articulated considerations of the national interest, but they differ substantially from those of other countries. In spite of the recent increase around the world in resistance to subsidies tied to industrial or development policies, countries that have used them do not want to see their policy freedoms restricted. The United States, for its part, wishes to maintain its right to the unrestrained use of countervailing duties.

The political foundation of the U.S. position has several pillars. There is the aforementioned equity and fairness argument that the playing field of international trade has become too tilted by government interventions of all sorts and that its level needs to be restored. Implicit in this position is the belief that U.S. subsidies are significantly lower and less distorting than those abroad. This is an argument that is widely disputed among America's trading partners.[10]

American policymakers and the industry groups that seek CVD protection believe that subsidies give foreign exporting firms unfair advantages. Countervailing duties are seen as a means of nullifying these advantages--at least as far as competition in the U.S. market is concerned. In many instances, the threat of a CVD action may be more valuable from the perspective of a petitioning firm or industry than its realization. This is the case whenever foreign producers targetted by the action agree to settle "out-of-court" and whenever such settlements increase the monopoly elements governing production and/or distribution. It is important to note

9   For useful reviews of U.S. policy in this area, see Finger, J. Michael, "Antidumping and Antisubsidy Measures," in Finger and Olechowski, *The Uruguay Round*; Finger, and Murray (1990); Hufbauer, G.C., and J. Shelton Erb, *Subsidies in International Trade*, IIE, 1984 and Jackson (1990).

10   In a recent study, for example, Gaisford and McLachlan (1990) compare "standardized" U.S. and Canadian subsidy rates at the federal level and find that the USA had higher rates in a large majority of the cases examined. They find further that "high (low) US industry subsidy rates [tended] to be paired with high (low) Canadian subsidy rates" (p. 64).

that commonly such negotiated settlements are advantageous to both domestic and foreign producers at the expense of consumers.

The possibility of such outcomes creates a non-trivial moral-hazard problem arising from incentives to file petitions which may be intrinsically frivolous, but which may nevertheless induce foreign producers to settle. It was, indeed, the desire to protect its producers from this kind of harassment that animated Canada's interest in developing procedures for prior notification, bilateral consultation, and bilateral dispute settlement.

For the countervailing as well as the subsidizing nation, therefore, the present system creates significant opportunities for abuse. Interest groups in the former can turn countervailing duties into protectionist barriers against imports,[11] while the policy process itself may encourage producers in both to attempt to cartelize the domestic market by means of VERs.

Regional vs. Multilateral Approaches

The uncertain future of many subsidy-CVD issues at the multilateral level of the GATT increases the importance of regional efforts to find workable solutions. This certainly includes the forthcoming talks among the three North American nations.[12] The significance of this effort is enhanced by the fact that a number of the most controversial U.S. CVD cases have involved Canada and Mexico. Examples include regional tire subsidies, alleged subsidized stumpage for timber in Canada, pricing of natural gas by Pemex, and the ceramic tile case of alleged subsidized official finance involving Mexico.[13] In the case of Mexico, moreover, questions regarding the treatment of infant-industry subsidies and of other interventions related

---

11 For recent summaries of the growing literature on the political economy of trade policy and the role of interest groups, see Baldwin, R.E., *The Political Economy of U.S. Import Policy*, (1985a); and Baldwin, R.E., "Trade Policies in Developed Countries," (1985b); Hillman, Arye L., *The Political Economy of Protection*, Harwood Academic Publishers, 1989; and Odell, John S., and Thomas D. Willett, *International Trade Policies*, Ann Arbor, MI: The University of Michigan Press, 1990.

12 See the useful summary of Uruguay Round negotiations on subsidy issues in Hufbauer (1990).

13 For further discussion of these and other cases, see Hufbauer and Erb (1984); Finger and Murray (1990); and Weintraub, S., *A Marriage of Convenience*, New York, NY: Oxford University Press, 1990. See also Siac, R.C., "The Use and Abuse of Unfair Trade Remedy Laws: The Mexican-U.S. Experience," Toronto: Centre for International Studies, January 1991.

to development policies, all issues which have been avoided by the GATT in the past, will complicate negotiations.

Bilateral and regional aspects of this issue are especially important in view of U.S. policy of applying MFN code treatment only on a conditional basis. Specifically, the USA has been willing to apply the material injury test for CVD actions only to countries which formally declare their intention to reduce subsidies. It is unclear to what extent this show of goodwill applies to all subsidies or only to the distorting kind. It means, however, that the USA has in effect adopted a country-specific approach to the issue of subsidies.

The Canadian-U.S. free trade negotiators were not able to reach agreement on a subsidies code,[14] in part because some believed that the problem was not amenable to bilateral resolution wherever competition from third parties was involved. Although further efforts are being expended to find bilateral solutions, this issue lies at the heart of the conflict between bilateral and multilateral approaches to trade liberalization and conflict resolution.[15]

This issue will be no less important in the upcoming North American negotiations. Agreements on subsidy-CVD issues might be difficult to achieve within a North American free trade area. A comprehensive agreement could, on the other hand, serve as a model for negotiation at the multilateral level. The possibility that aspects of the USA-Canada agreement might serve as role models to the world at large was indeed one of the great hopes of the talks at their beginning.

Points of Contention

A number of key analytical issues have arisen in the context of disputes over subsidies and CVD policies.[16] One is the need to develop better criteria for identifying subsidies that are most troublesome or distortive of

---

14   See Schott and Smith (1988) and Wonnacott, Paul, *The United States and Canada: The Quest for Free Trade*, Washington, DC: Institute for International Economics, 1985.

15   For recent treatments of these issues see Arndt, S.W., and Thomas D. Willett, "EC 1992 From a North American Perspective," *Economic Journal*, Vol. 101, No. 409, November 1991; and Schott (1989) and the references cited there.

16   For more detailed discussions, see Balassa, B., "Subsidies and Countervailing Measures: Economic Considerations," *Journal of World Trade*, 23 J.W.T. 2, 73, 1989; Gaisford and McLachlan (1990); Hufbauer and Erb (1984) and Hufbauer (1990).

international trade. There is fairly broad consensus on the desirability of distinguishing between generally available and thus non-actionable subsidies and subsidies targetted for particular types of enterprises and hence more likely to be discriminatory and economically difficult to justify. One of the problems in implementing such a distinction, however, is that even subsidies that are advertised as generally available, may in practice be restricted to particular targetted firms or industries.

In cases of subsidies designed to offset existing distortions, Hufbauer and Erb have proposed that countries' market shares of the products affected be used to replace the current distinction in the international subsidies code between industrial subsidies in developed and developing countries. This is an intriguing idea, which has not received the detailed analysis needed to evaluate its attractiveness.

Natural resource pricing, the use of regional development and structural adjustment programs, and policies to encourage high-tech industries represent applications of subsidy policies that have created conflicts among countries. Questions have arisen with respect to both their status as non-actionable subsidies and the function of international oversight. In addition to the institutional problems involved in such oversight, procedural issues arise with respect to burden of proof, fact-finding, legal rulings, and dispute settlement.

A further source of disagreement pertains to the warranted size of a countervailing duty. When both parties to a dispute subsidize the same industry, the warranted countervailing duty is at best the difference between the two subsidies, in which case it may have to be negative if the subsidy in the countervailing country is higher. While the USA does tend to subsidize less than most countries, the patterns of subsidization vary considerably from one industry to another. Differences in points of view about the appropriate definition of industries and treatment of indirect subsidies can yield substantial variations in the calculations.

Furthermore, as Gaisford and McLachlan (1990) have shown, the answer becomes even more complicated in a world of multiple subsidies, multiple products, some of which may be inputs and/or non-tradable, and multiple factors of production. Under such circumstances, the notion, so dear to petitioners and policymakers alike, that a countervailing duty inevitably furthers the particular as well as the national interest quickly breaks down.

Alternative Strategies

As already noted, a serious shortcoming of U.S. policy is the frequent resort to VERs as the ultimate "resolution" of a CVD dispute. While avoidance of VERs and of negotiated price floors runs the risk of increasing international conflicts over CVD policies, their economic costs justify efforts to reduce their use. Outright prohibition of such measures may be too extreme, especially if political feasibility is considered. But sharp curtailment of their use is not difficult to justify.

Although such a policy revision could be directly implemented at the executive level of the U.S. government, some type of legislative action would doubtless be both desirable and required.[17] What form such action should take and whether it could be sold to Congress are questions that deserve careful attention. Part of the answer surely rests in ensuring more complete understanding of the full implications of CVDs. In addition to the issues raised above, policymakers and the public would have to be made aware of the fact that in a resource-constrained world a foreign subsidy which draws resources into one industry is more than likely pulling them out of another, so that a subsidy-induced increase in the other country's exports also increases its imports.

Similarly, a CVD which helps to increase employment and capital accumulation in one industry more than likely reduces both in one or more others. The strongly entrenched tendency to treat each countervailable duty as if it were the only intervention and entirely disconnected from all other policies is likely, upon examination, to be the source of a great many policy errors.

The propensity to settle CVD issues by means of VERs is an example of policy myopia from the standpoint of national efficiency concerns.[18] Given the tendency for VERs to reduce foreign opposition to domestic trade policy actions, it would be desirable to couple curtailment of the use of

---

17   There is a precedent for such legislation in Section 604 of the Trade and Tariff Act of 1984 which requires that for termination of a CVD investigation because of agreements with foreign governments to limit the exports in question, the Commerce Department must conclude that the agreement is in the public interest, taking into account specified factors which include whether the agreement would have a larger negative impact on U.S. consumers than the imposition of CVDs. See Bello, Judith Hippler, and Alan F. Holmer, *The Antidumping and Countervailing Duty Laws: Legal and Policy Issues*, Washington, DC: American Bar Association, 1987, pp. 114-15.

18   The origin of such policies may, of course, lie as much or more in catering to special interests as in actual myopia on the part of government officials.

VERs with reduction in the U.S. propensity to undertake CVD actions. One step in this direction, which has been proposed by several economists (including Balassa, 1989; Gaisford and McLachlan, 1990 and Wonnacott, 1985) is to increase the *de minimis* rate of foreign subsidization needed to trigger a U.S. policy response from the current 0.5% to, say, 1.0%. This proposal is based on the presumption that material injury would be unlikely to follow from subsidies below this rate. While the 1.0% level (to say nothing of the 0.5% level) is arbitrary, it would limit the number of CVD cases to some extent, provided that subsidizing nations do not respond by increasing the size of their subsidies.

Perhaps the potentially most important improvement would be to change the current injury provisions from a gross to a net definition. This would reflect the spirit of Finger's (1987) proposal that the injury determination process should involve not only domestic producers of goods which compete with subsidized imports, but the consumers of those goods. This change would recognize the existence of other legitimate interests. Just as domestic import-competing firms can suffer injury from foreign subsidization, domestic consumers suffer injuries from CVD and VER policies. Accounting for consumer interests in the injury determination process, that is, evaluating injury on an economy-wide basis, would substantially reduce the number of cases yielding a positive determination of injury.

Careful attention should be given to possible ways of implementing this suggestion. For example, the ITC, USTR, or the Council of Economic Advisers could be assigned the task of preparing estimates of costs to the economy which would accompany the imposition of particular CVDs. The adoption of a true test of net injury might well not prove to be politically saleable, but almost any movement in the direction of accounting properly for the costs of CVD actions for the rest of the economy would be helpful.

One advantage of this approach is that it would focus attention on strategic trade policy situations in which foreign subsidies are harmful to the overall economic interests of a country. Most typically, these would be situations involving the subsidization of high tech industries. As Hufbauer and Erb (1984, pp. 119-20) note, in such cases simply offsetting the foreign subsidy with a CVD would in all likelihood be insufficient to remove the competitive advantage which had been secured by foreign producers.

In such circumstances, direct negotiation with the foreign government, buttressed by the possibility of a countervailing domestic action, seems likely to be the best strategy. The greater the degree of international agreement which can be secured on rules of the game with respect to subsidies for strategic industries, the less conflictual will be relations in this area. While efforts to resolve these disagreements must continue at the level of the GATT, it is also highly desirable to pursue the issue at regional levels, including the North American. Greater use of formal dispute settlement procedures is also desirable in cases where negotiated agreements cannot be reached. Indeed, a strong emphasis on such dispute settlement mechanisms would be one method of introducing a net injury test into policy practice.

As a potential model for more comprehensive agreements, the treatment of these issues within the context of a North American free trade agreement would seem to have a substantial advantage over the bilateral negotiations between the United States and Canada. The tripartite discussions would bring to the table countries at different stages of development, while still benefitting from the small number of negotiating parties and the other intangible attributes which make regional arrangements so popular. An important issue between developed and developing countries concerns the extent to which infant and strategic industry subsidies adopted by developing countries require international surveillance and control.

Countervailing Subsidies in Place of Duties

Hufbauer and Erb (1984) have suggested countervailing subsidies as an alternative to countervailing duties in order to account properly for the *consumer benefits* inherent in foreign subsidies. Replacement of a duty with a subsidy retains the output effect of the former, without impairing the consumer benefits inherent in subsidized imports. In this way, consumers continue to enjoy the benefits of lower prices, while domestic producers are protected from output and employment losses.

The countervailing subsidy does, however, entail an outlay on the part of the importing country's government. It still leaves incentives for foreign and domestic firms to reach market-restricting negotiated settlements prior to final determination of injury and hence of the countervailing subsidy. Indeed, importing country governments may have greater incentives to encourage negotiated settlements in order to avoid the outlays associated with countervailing subsidies.

In order to minimize budget costs to the importing country, Hufbauer and Erb suggest that countervailing subsidies be financed by low rates of duty on all imports originating in the subsidizing country. By imposing costs on many foreign export industries, this approach has the additional advantage of generating incentives against the use of targetted subsidies.

A potentially serious problem, however, is that there could develop considerable mismatches between the levels of foreign and domestic subsidies. To match a given per unit foreign subsidy, as implied by the philosophy of our current CVD laws, but shown to lead to erroneous forms of intervention in many cases, relatively little revenue would be required for a small domestic industry, while considerable revenues might be required if the domestic industry were large. Especially in the latter case, it seems questionable whether the subsidy approach would promote overall economic efficiency. Further technical analysis is required to determine the conditions under which countervailing subsidies would be preferable to countervailing duties. While the CVS proposal is intriguing, it seems at best a second-best solution to the subsidy-CVD problem.

Rebating CVD Revenues

Gaisford and McLachlan (1990) have recently offered a proposal just the reverse of Hufbauer and Erb's. Their proposal calls for a rebate of CVD tariff revenue to the subsidizing nation. It is based on the notion that the revenue gained through the imposition of CVDs comes as a windfall to the countervailing nation and represents an unwarranted incentive encouraging the use of CVDs.

A rebate of this type may be viewed as a side payment, and as such might have two unfortunate consequences. First, the original subsidizing nation obtains additional revenues with which to break fiscal constraints on subsidization. Since, as Hufbauer notes (1990, p. 94), this fiscal constraint has become increasingly binding of late, the proposal to rebate CVD revenues might encourage greater use of subsidies. Second, eliminating the incentive on the part of the responding nation to apply CVDs without reducing the ease with which actions can be brought would encourage the use of cartelized export restraints as an alternative to CVDs.

If we interpret subsidized imports as creating an externality, then it is possible to apply the Coase theorem (1960) to the subsidy-CVD issue.[19] The Coase theorem suggests that if property rights are well established, with respect to the right of a sovereign state to subsidize or countervail, then externalities can be internalized in an economically efficient manner through the use of appropriate side payments. For example, if the USA finds evidence of injury from a Mexican subsidy, one policy solution would be for the U.S. government to make a *side payment* to the Mexican Government--the real creator of the externality as opposed to the exporting firm--to abandon the subsidy policy.

---

19   Coase, R., "The Problem of Social Cost," *Journal of Law and Economics*, 1960.

At some point, the benefits to Mexico from subsidization would be less than the side payment from the USA and a change in policy would be effected. Alternatively, if a countervailing duty is settled upon as an appropriate policy in the USA, but that CVD causes some *external harm* to Mexico, then Mexico might make a side payment to the injured firm in the USA if it wishes to maintain its export subsidy.

Coasian side payments between states would eliminate the firm-to-firm negotiations that currently bring about much of the harm generated by the subsidy-CVD process. Since the subsidizing country government, not the subsidized firm, *is responsible for the externality*, it is best to focus on a change of country policy, not firm behaviour.

Third-Country Effects and Complications in the Coasian Approach

In many subsidy cases, there are more parties involved than just the exporting and importing countries. Other countries which export to the same market might see their interests affected. For instance, suppose both Canada and Mexico export some good to the U.S. Canadian production subsidies on exports to the USA not only affect competing American firms, but Mexican exporters to the USA. A system of state-to-state side payments could address the claims of all injured parties. Although an increase in the number of parties involved increases the difficulty of reaching an efficient Coasian solution, this may still be an attractive way of handling major third country effects since current CVD policies are poorly suited to deal with such issues.[20]

Although the Coasian approach to these issues offers some interesting possibilities, some important political economy considerations may hinder its practical applicability. Given the conflicting views about the objective of policy with respect to subsidy-CVD issues, it could be quite difficult to secure agreement on an initial assignment of "property rights" with respect to the rights to subsidize and the rights to engage in CVD activities. In the absence of a clear assignment of property rights, Coasian bargaining will not always lead to agreement.

Furthermore, with the explicit or implicit establishment of the wrong set of property rights, the ability of special interests to collude could be enhanced. Thus, in VER negotiations, for example, the implicit recognition of the property rights of foreign firms to export to the USA and of U.S. firms' rights to be protected from foreign competition has combined to

---

20   See, for example, Hufbauer and Erb (1984, pp. 117-18).

undermine consumers' rights to free imports and has resulted in the adoption of particularly damaging cartelizing measures. While the resulting aggregate costs to consumers far exceed the gains generated for domestic and foreign producers, the large number of consumers presents traditional collective action problems which prevents their bribing producers to give up their restrictive practices. In such large-number cases, where transactions costs are significant, the simple Coase theorem that economic efficiency is not influenced by the distribution of property rights does not hold. Thus recognition of the possibilities of Coasian bargaining doesn't relieve us of the necessity to clearly define rights to trade (and to limit trade).[21]

Conclusions

The intractability of the subsidy-CVD issue is in part a conceptual and analytical matter and in part one of policy and practice. The conceptual problem is to identify harmful and distorting subsidies and to select from those subsidies that are harmful to the interests of other countries. A related and no less important matter is to evaluate the costs and effectiveness of alternative antidotes.

The practical problem is to devise criteria and rules for international intervention in the case of subsidies that warrant such intervention on grounds of principle. Guidelines and procedures are needed for subsidies that warrant international concern. Among the key requirements here is the formulation of guidelines not only for countries wishing to subsidize, but for those resorting to countervailing policies. Legal and institutional mechanisms are needed for international surveillance, enforcement, and dispute settlement.

National governments have at present too much discretion in the use of both subsidies and countervailing measures. Although the GATT has something to say about both (in Articles VI and XVI and in various Tracks of the Subsidies Code), see Jackson (1990) for details. The guidelines are ambiguous and weak and not supported by adequate compliance and dispute settlement procedures.

---

21   Attention also needs to be given to the proper form of side payments, since implementation of such payments has proven to be particularly difficult in international regulations. On the use of issue linkages as a substitute for side payments in international negotiations, see Tollison, R., and Thomas D. Willett, "An Economic Theory of Mutually Advantageous Issue Linkages in International Negotiations," *International Organization*, Autumn, 1979.

U.S. policy on countervailing duties is confused and muddled. Policymakers rarely know the full implications of foreign subsidies for U.S. interests and when they know, existing law prevents them from acting intelligently on that information. U.S. producers of import-competing goods have been allowed to view CVDs as entitlements; they have utilized that privilege to collude with foreigners in introducing monopolistic distortions into many markets.

On political economy grounds, the trend to circumvent formal procedures through the negotiation of voluntary restraints is quite understandable. By facilitating monopolistic restrictions, protection of domestic producers is kept from harming influential foreign producers. As a result, dangers of retaliation are substantially reduced and strains on international relations are lessened. But such "cooperative protectionism" is imposing heavy costs on consumers and the overall efficiency of the economy. Efforts to put a halt to such negotiated market cartelizations need not wait for resolution of the full range of analytical complexities in the delineation of optimal CVD policies.

Improvements in CVD policies, however, are unlikely to be forthcoming without greater agreement on the role of subsidies. The difficulty of that undertaking is amply illustrated by the failure of the USA and Canada to reach agreement on a subsidies code, and this in spite of the predominance between the two countries of similar traditions and perspectives on the issue. All the same, Canada could not overcome the constraint inherent in the greater policy role of subsidies at both the federal and provincial levels. The differences in the weights attached to subsidy use in national economic strategies in the case of the USA and Mexico are, of course, several times greater and hence may be even harder to reconcile.

There is, moreover, a legitimate question regarding the suitability of bilateral or regional arrangements for the resolution of disagreements over subsidies. An important advantage favouring bilaterals would seem to rest in the small number of players relative to multilateral forums within the GATT. On the other hand, a deal with a single trading partner is unattractive because it limits the reciprocal benefits a country obtains for reducing its subsidies in comparison with the gains implicit in a reciprocal arrangement involving many countries. The relative weights of these considerations would vary among industries and would depend on the importance to Canada and Mexico of competition with other subsidizing countries and on the magnitude of foreign industrial subsidies.

Given that subsidies are more extensive in Canada (and even more so in Mexico) than in the United States, many Canadians believed not only that they would gain relatively little from bilateral resolution of this issue, but also that any reduction in domestic subsidies would place Canadian producers at competitive disadvantages vis-à-vis third countries.

The political economy in this context is such that economists' claims that the inherently welfare-reducing impact of many subsidies implies that even unilateral--that is, unreciprocated--elimination of subsidies would be beneficial does not carry very far. Far more important in convincing Canadians of the value of a bilateral agreement would be the expectation of greater constraints on U.S. CVD policies.

In the end, however, the USA and Canada agreed merely to continue their talks on a new subsidies code for several more years and to establish in the meanwhile a bilateral panel for the review of administrative agency findings under the application of the respective national laws. Unable to agree on a new code, they provided for improved dispute settlement procedures pertaining to the application of national law.

The importance of bringing Mexico into these negotiations is clear, for any USA-Canada agreement on a new subsidies code would benefit Mexico. The need to extract reciprocal concessions from Mexico is viewed as especially important in light of Mexico's long history and relatively aggressive use of subsidies.[22]

Mexico has recently rewritten its subsidy code to conform more closely with U.S. law.[23] While this should facilitate regional negotiations of a new code, Mexico unlike Canada has little experience in the administration of codes of this type. Furthermore, subsidies embedded in Mexico's federal budget have drawn criticism, but similar charges can easily be addressed to the United States and Canada. Although parastatals and other enterprises targetted by state policies have traditionally been major recipients of domestic subsidies, Mexico has in the years since the inception of the current program of economic reforms substantially reduced the role of parastatals through privatization. Still, a key issue needing resolution concerns subsidies embedded in the pricing structures of the remaining parastatals, especially those in the energy sector, to ensure either the removal of such subsidies or their "general availability" to American and Canadian users. The complexity of the task is readily apparent, not least because limiting general availability to North American users may run afoul

---

22   On this issue, see Morici, P., *Trade Talks with Mexico: A Time for Realism*, Washington, DC: National Planning Association, 1991.

23   See U.S. International Trade Commission, *Review of Trade and Investment Liberalization Measures by Mexico and Prospects for Future United States-Mexican Relations*, Washington, DC: April 1990.

of the spirit if not the letter of the GATT's most-favoured-nation clause. If, on the other hand, general availability is applied to third countries, the competitive value of the agreement to the USA and Canada is correspondingly reduced.

Chapter 6

Dealing with Nontariff Barriers in a Trilateral Free Trade Agreement

Murray G. Smith[1]

Introduction

This paper examines how nontariff barriers may be dealt with in the trilateral North American Free Trade negotiations involving Mexico, the United States and Canada. Available from the authors is an appendix, which reviews many of the nontariff barriers applied by Canada, the United States and Mexico that affect trilateral trade.

The first section of the paper summarizes briefly a classification of nontariff barriers. The paper then discusses factors influencing the agenda for the NAFTA negotiations including the linkage between the trilateral negotiations and the Uruguay Round of GATT negotiations and considers some of the issues which have acquired particular prominence in the trilateral negotiations, specifically trade restrictions imposed on environmental grounds. Finally, the paper deals with the issue of how either substantive rules or procedural processes might be developed to address some of the main nontariff barriers present between the three countries.

1   I wish to acknowledge the capable research assistance of James Nickel and Denis Pacquin. An appendix is available from the author detailing North American subsidies and non-tariff barriers.

Classification of Nontariff Barriers

The main nontariff barriers can be grouped as follows:
1. Border Measures
   a) quotas and licenses
   b) customs valuation
   c) export subsidies and drawback
   d) rules of origin
   e) phytosanitary and technical inspections
2. Trade Laws
   a) antidumping and countervailing duties and procedures
   b) safeguard actions
3. Internal Measures
   a) procurement preferences
   b) intellectual property issues
   c) domestic subsidies
   f) performance requirements

This classification of nontariff measures affecting trade would be widely accepted in international trade negotiations. Indeed all of these issues were addressed in the Canada-USA Free Trade negotiations, although in the end there was no agreement on intellectual property issues in those negotiations. This paper does not address the issues of barriers to the mobility of direct investment or labour among the three economies. The latter are most often barriers to trade in services, although these barriers to factor mobility may also impede trade in goods.

Other domestic policies or regulatory measures may be viewed as having an effect on the pattern of trade. The most prominent such issues associated with the trilateral Free Trade negotiations are domestic environmental policies. Certainly, the debate in the U.S. Congress in the first half of 1991 over the extension of the fast track negotiating authority focused attention on environmental policies in Mexico as well as raising other issues such as labour standards.

The Negotiating Agenda for a North American Free Trade Agreement

The rules and procedures for dealing with nontariff barriers in a trilateral North American Free Trade Agreement will be influenced by the overall architecture of the NAFTA and its relationship to the existing Canada-USA Free Trade Agreement. In addition the NAFTA negotiations will interact with the final stages of the Uruguay Round of GATT negotiations because there is substantial overlap in the agendas for the two sets of negotiations.

Linkages to the Uruguay Round and the Multilateral Trading System

The uncertainties about the outcome of the Uruguay Round after the impasse at the Brussels Ministerial complicate the intra-North American agenda greatly. It appears that there is a vague consensus among the three countries that it would be very convenient if the most difficult issues-- agricultural subsidies and trade barriers, textiles trade restrictions, trade rules for subsidies and countervailing and antidumping duties, government procurement practices, and rules for intellectual property--were resolved through the multilateral process. Although an impasse in the multilateral negotiations will reinforce interest in regional trading arrangements, the failure to deal with these more difficult issues as well as more prosaic issues such as multilateral tariff reductions, will make the substantive negotiations among the United States, Mexico and Canada much more difficult.

On the specific issue of rules for subsidies and countervailing duties, Canada's interest in trilateral negotiation of those issues will be influenced by the continuing experience with the operation of the Chapter 19 appeal mechanism for the antidumping and countervailing duty laws and procedures; the outcome of the Uruguay Round negotiations on subsidies and countervailing duties; the outcome of the Uruguay Round agriculture negotiations, and the unresolved issues about softwood lumber.

The outcome of the Uruguay Round will also be significant for the potential trade diversion consequences of Mexico's recent free trade initiative. It is evident that the potential for trade diversion in a free trade agreement involving Mexico and the United States, or the United States and Canada is significant because Mexico is a low wage complementary economy. Of course, the potential for trade diversion derives from Canadian and U.S. trade barriers. For example, Mexico is not a major supplier of textiles and apparel products to Canada, but because Canada imposes high tariffs and bilateral restraints on low-cost suppliers under the Multifiber Arrangement, Mexico might expand substantially exports of these products if it was exempted from these Canadian trade barriers. If, however, significant liberalization of tariff and nontariff barriers to textiles and apparel trade can be achieved in the Uruguay Round, then the potential for trade diversion will be reduced.

Trade Restrictions Derived From Environmental Concerns

Environmental issues loomed large in the debate in the U.S. Congress about the extension of negotiating authority for the Free Trade negotiations with Mexico, but the relationship between achieving environmental objectives and the obligations, which could be included in a North American free trade agreement, remains uncertain.

Until recently, most of the trade restrictions countries have imposed on environmental grounds have involved phytosanitary standards. The Canada-USA FTA has put in place a mechanism to deal with phytosanitary issues but the appropriateness of this mechanism for the trilateral negotiations needs to be considered. The objective established in the Canada-USA FTA was to achieve voluntary harmonization of standards in specific products such as veterinary medicines, but progress has been extremely limited.

More importantly new types of issues have arisen because of trade restrictions imposed on environmental grounds. It is interesting to note that the first two cases under the Chapter 18 dispute settlement process of the Canada-USA FTA--the Canadian landing requirements for salmon and herring and the U.S. size requirements for lobsters--involved the interpretation of the exceptions in GATT Article XX. Similarly Mexico has launched a GATT complaint about U.S restrictions upon imports of tuna.

Before considering these issues in detail it is useful to review the relevant GATT rules pertaining to environmental measures. The key provisions in the GATT involve the concept of national treatment as applied to domestic regulations, the GATT provisions regarding technical standards, and the special exceptions in the GATT relating to protection of "human, animal or plant" health and the conservation of exhaustible resources.

First, in the General Agreement itself there is a commitment under Article III of the GATT to national treatment. The concept of national treatment is simple--it means that imported products receive treatment that is no less favourable than that afforded domestic products--but the concept is frequently misunderstood. Certainly there were many misunderstandings of this concept in the debate in Canada over the Free Trade Agreement (FTA) with the United States. The Free Trade Agreement has simply incorporated GATT Article III as the national treatment obligation governing trade in goods.

The GATT rules pertaining to standards have evolved incrementally over decades. The main provision is the application of national treatment to product standards. The only other provision in the GATT (under the General Agreement itself), that applies to standards is Article X where there is an observation that countries should publish and notify all regulations of commerce including those related to standards, to deceptive business practices or other related issues. And there is an obligation under Article X which states that countries "shall administer in a uniform, impartial and reasonable manner all its laws, regulations decisions and rulings." Moreover, it is suggested that this obligation extends to delegated authorities including private non-governmental standards authorities.

Note that there are no obligations in the GATT to harmonize standards. Countries are permitted to impose different or more stringent standards if they so choose. However, the national treatment obligation means that the standards must be applied in a non-discriminatory fashion to domestic and imported products.

During the Tokyo Round, there was a recognition by all the trading countries that technical barriers were a growing and very significant set of nontariff barriers to trade. In particular, there was an effort to negotiate a standards code in the Tokyo Round to create some more precise rules governing standards and to limit the extent to which they could be nontariff barriers to trade. The code, entitled the *Agreement on Technical Barriers to Trade*, that was agreed during the Tokyo Round recognizes in the preamble, "that no country should be prevented from taking measures necessary to ensure the quality of its exports or for the protection of human, animal or plant life or health, of the environment or for the prevention of deceptive practices." So again the general exception that was in the GATT is incorporated, and indeed extended by the explicit reference to the environment in the Technical Barriers code. What the technical barriers code sought to do in particular in extending the GATT rules, is to formalize and regularize certification procedures. In particular, there are obligations under Article 5 of the Technical Barriers code that seek to make certification procedures as non-discriminatory as possible, and it is quite clear under Article 6 of the technical barriers code that this obligation extends to local government bodies and non-governmental bodies who are determining technical regulations or standards.

Clearly the issue of phytosanitary standards is among the more contentious today both in the GATT negotiations and in the implementation of the Free Trade Agreement. The Free Trade Agreement stresses developing compatibility of standards and mutual recognition of standards and testing procedures between Canada and the United States, while taking account of international standardization efforts. What the Free Trade Agreement does is set out some principles to govern phytosanitary standards and sets up a work program to seek mutual recognition of standards. Again this is cast in terms of the very limited, carefully measured obligations

Table 1
U.S. Phytosanitary and Environmental Barriers to Mexican Exports

Avocado (banned in 1940's)	alleged worm in seed
Cajahta (goat's milk--cheese)	application of milk quota
Mango	fruit fly/hot water for 90 minutes
Lemon/Orange/Grapefruit	citrus canker
Tomatoes	marketing orders
China/pottery	limits on lead and cadmium
Eggs	sampling for salmonella
Chicken	Newcastle disease
Chilies	banned for pesticides
Potato	Nematodes
Tuna	restrictions under Marine Mammals Protection Act because dolphins are killed by harvests
Shrimp	restrictions because turtles are killed in shrimp harvest

which have characterized previous GATT obligations with respect to standards. This obligation in the Canada-USA FTA, however, became an issue during the free trade debate. There was a comic book circulated among the Canadian public which suggested that the effect of the Free Trade Agreement would be to lead to an influx of American chickens which are inferior to Canadian chickens and potentially prejudicial to the health of Canadians. Of course, quite apart from misrepresenting standards issues, this comic book did not take account of the fact that the Canadian marketing boards would remain in effect and that Canada's import quotas on chickens would remain.

The difficult policy issues today with respect to standards frequently are questions that cannot be dealt with very effectively under the existing GATT rules, but they are questions of taste in the sense of determining what is the appropriate level of standards and whether those standards should be higher or lower. There is a Latin proverb, *de gustibus non disputandum*, which can be rendered very loosely as "one cannot argue about questions of taste." In fact when it comes to product standards and environmental standards, there are all sorts of grounds for arguments about issues of taste.

Furthermore, there are exceptions permitted in the GATT to the basic obligations such as national treatment such as the Provisional Protocol of Application. Existing legislative derogations from GATT rules were "grandfathered." For example Canada still claims grandfather rights for the Canadian regulations governing the colouring of margarine under the Provisional Protocol of Application.

More important, and perhaps more interesting, are the exceptions under Article XX of the GATT. These exceptions include the ones that provide for "the conservation of exhaustible resources" and those regulations "necessary to protect human, animal or plant life or health." Therefore, under this latter provision a wide variety of environmental, phytosanitary and other issues are now considered to be an exception under the GATT rules of Article XX. The first dispute settlement case under the Free Trade Agreement, which involved Canada's landing requirement on herring and salmon, pertains to the interpretation of the exceptions under Article XX of the GATT and this is the key issue in the trade dispute between Mexico and the United States over the restrictions on the importation of tuna.

The issue arising in the tuna case is whether an importing jurisdiction can impose an import restriction, because there is a perceived adverse environmental impact from the production process utilized in the exporting jurisdiction. It seems clear that Article XX of the GATT permits considerable latitude for import restrictions when there is an alleged threat to "human, animal or plant life or health" in the importing jurisdiction, but the exception does not appear to extend to extraterritorial policing of the environmental impact of production processes.

The U.S. administration has prepared an action plan to deal with environmental issues between Mexico and the United States on separate track from the trilateral free trade negotiations. This plan involves several elements including increased resources for USA-Mexico transboundary pollution and modest financial assistance for Mexico's environmental agency to enhance its enforcement capabilities. Although such voluntary cooperation on environmental issues is clearly desirable, it may also be necessary to address the issue of trade rules pertaining to environmental measures.

Negotiating Approaches

This section examines possible approaches to negotiating nontariff barriers in the trilateral North American Free Trade negotiations. The negotiations on border measures and on the trade laws are linked to the outcome of negotiations on domestic measures such as subsidies, procurement preferences and environmental regulation.

Negotiating Border Measures

The stated goal of the trilateral negotiations is to achieve a comprehensive North American free trade agreement, which would eventually eliminate tariffs and export duties among the three economies. In this respect the NAFTA would parallel the Canada-USA Free Trade Agreement, but the timetable for tariff reductions could be slower and the rules of origin for a NAFTA could differ from the Canada-USA FTA.

It is customary in free trade areas to eliminate duty drawbacks for exports qualifying for preferred access to the markets of free trade partners. Thus duty drawbacks and waivers are eliminated by January 1, 1994 in the Canada-USA Free Trade Agreement. Although Mexico might seek a longer transition period, duty drawback--known as maquiladora in Mexico--would almost certainly disappear in a NAFTA.

One obvious element of the negotiation of a trilateral free trade agreement will be the rules of origin. The pressure for restrictive rules of origin is greater in industries characterized by significant nontariff barriers to trade. Moreover, rules of origin in themselves can become significant nontariff barriers to trade. It is important that the trilateral NAFTA have clear and transparent rules of origin in order that compliance costs and administrative discretion are minimized. The existing Canada-USA Free Trade Agreement utilizes primarily a change of tariff classification criteria to determine substantial transformation. However, assembly activities have a 50 percent direct cost of manufacturing requirement which may be subject to some degree of ambiguity in measurement and administration. Restrictive rules of origin can frustrate the benefits of the removal of trade barriers.

The potential interaction between a trilateral FTA and the existing Canada-USA FTA can be illustrated by reference to a particular industrial sector which will be a central focus of concern during the trilateral negotiations, namely the automotive sector. It appears that the United States will press for a restrictive rule of origin for trade in automotive products under the trilateral Free Trade Agreement. From a trade policy perspective it is puzzling why the United States with a tariff of 2.5 percent on automotive products currently, and an MFN tariff that will be even lower after completion of the Uruguay Round, would care very much about the rules of origin for automotive products because the potential incentives for trade diversion or trade deflection are extremely limited with such a low MFN USA tariff. However, the economic impact and political clout of the automotive sector is such that the rules for this sector will receive great scrutiny in the Congress. Of course, parts of Canada will also attach considerable interest to the outcome in the particular sector.

For its part, Canada is likely to continue to resist restrictive rules of origin in the automotive sector, in part because of concerns about the impact on Japanese assembly plants in Canada which are already facing the elimination of duty remission by 1993 under the existing terms of a Canada-USA Free Trade Agreement. Increasing the rule of origin requirement under the existing Canada-USA Free Trade Agreement or the trilateral Free Trade Agreement will raise some concerns in Canada. Thus, if the trilateral Free Trade Agreement has more restrictive rules of origin on the automotive sector then the Japanese transplants may prefer to qualify under the existing more liberal rules of origin under the Canada-USA Free Trade Agreement. Even when the trilateral agreement's phase-ins are fully implemented, trade may still occur under the rules of the bilateral Canada-USA Free Trade Agreement because the rules of origin may be less restrictive in the bilateral agreement.

In addition to the rules of origin for preferential tariff access, the other key issue for border measures under NAFTA will be the coverage of quotas and import licenses. In principle, all such quantitative restrictions should be eliminated, but there will be pressures to retain, at least for a considerable period, many of these quantitative restrictions.

The issue of restrictive rules of origin and the retention of quantitative restrictions on imports often are closely linked. Both Canada and the United States maintain extensive restraints on imports of textiles and clothing from low-cost countries.[2] As a result of concerns, especially on the U.S. side,

---

2   See Smith, Murray G., and Jean-François Bence, "Tariff Equivalents for Bilateral Export Restraints on Canada's Textile and Apparel Trade," Background Paper prepared for the Canada International Trade Tibunal Enquiry Into Textiles Tariffs, September 1989.

about the potential for trade diversion involving apparel made from offshore fabrics, special more restrictive rules of origin for apparel were included in the Canada-USA FTA. Canada does not impose MFA restraints on Mexico, presumably because competitive pressures are not intense, but the United States does impose extensive restraints on Mexican apparel exports. Liberalization of textiles and apparel trade on a multilateral basis, may increase short-term concerns about adjustment to import competition in the United States and Canada, but could also ease pressures for restrictive rules of origin for trilateral trade in this sector.

Much of Mexico's remaining import licenses and most of the quotas of Canada and the United States are concentrated in the agricultural sector. Clearly the outcome of the Uruguay Round negotiations on agricultural subsidies and trade barriers will set the parameters for the trilateral negotiations. Neither the United States nor Canada were prepared to reduce domestic agricultural subsidies in the Canada-USA Free Trade negotiations because of concerns about the impact of EC and Japanese agricultural policies. For its part, Mexico is going to be reluctant to dismantle its restrictions on imports of corn, grains and lentils, because millions of small farmers depend upon these products particularly while the United States and Canada retain substantial agricultural subsidies. Thus the retention of some import controls will be linked to the provision of domestic subsidies.

Negotiating Trade Laws

As part of the comprehensive negotiations on a Canada-USA trade agreement, a number of approaches to the more specific negotiations on import relief laws were suggested. These included:
- Granting national treatment of goods and services originating in the other country. National treatment means that foreign producers receive the same treatment under legislation and public policies as is afforded domestic producers. In practical terms, this amounts to the two countries' being exempted from the application of each other's import relief laws.
- Negotiating revised criteria for bilateral import relief measures.
- Maintaining bilateral import relief laws, but administering them jointly with the objective of limiting their bilateral application.
- Retaining separate national import relief systems, but introducing procedural changes in each country's domestic process and new standards of injury determination.

This section examines the main concerns that import relief laws address--dumping by private firms, and government subsidies, and examines how the various negotiating approaches could be used to resolve some of the central negotiating issues.

Dumping

The most contentious private business practice that import relief laws govern is dumping. In its strictest sense, dumping involves selling goods in the export market at a price that is lower than that at which the same goods are sold in the domestic market. In the domestic market, this is referred to as price discrimination, which is often linked to predatory pricing behaviour. The legal definition of dumping also refers to import prices that are below the full cost of production, regardless of whether dumping--in the sense of price discrimination--actually occurs.

Subsidies

Domestic subsidies are used by all three governments. Mexican subsidies have declined in recent years as privatization of state-owned enterprises has proceeded and the remaining subsidies are focused on consumer subsidies which are a form of income redistribution.[3] Detailed analysis of federal subsidies in Canada and the United States in an earlier study indicates that agricultural subsidies are substantial in Canada and the United States, but nonagricultural subsidies are modest and declining in both countries.[4]

National Treatment

Various negotiating approaches to antidumping duties are possible, but it is the national treatment, or bilateral exemption, option that makes the most logical sense. Removing tariff barriers and other nontariff barriers which segment national markets, removes the potential for predatory dumping based on a protected home market. Furthermore, eliminating antidumping procedures also would remove some of the potential for harassment of trade between the two countries.

Exempting bilateral trade completely from antidumping duties and procedures is feasible, at least in principle, because each country has domestic laws directed against unfair pricing. The exemption would involve

---

3   See an unpublished paper prepared by Cecilia Siac for the C.D. Howe Institute for an analysis of trends in Mexican subsidies.

4   See Smith and Bence (1989).

each country affording national treatment in the application of price discrimination laws.[5] Here is how this would work. If a company in Cleveland sells a product in its local market at a higher price than its sells that product in Hamilton, then the company would be subject to Canadian price discrimination laws. If the same company sells a product at a lower price in the Buffalo market, then it would be subject to U.S. price discrimination laws. If antidumping duties were eliminated, domestic price discrimination laws, such as Robinson-Patman in the United States and Section 34 of the *Competition Act* in Canada, still would apply and would provide remedies against pricing practices that could seriously damage competition.

Economists and U.S. jurists have criticized price discrimination laws in recent years because these laws can limit price competition that is not predatory and that is beneficial to society.[6] Canada has seldom used price discrimination laws. In the United States, recent rends in antitrust policy and enforcement have permitted firms greater flexibility in pricing strategies and have reduced the likelihood that price discounts will be sanctioned under price discrimination laws.

In both countries, trends in the enforcement of antidumping laws on the one hand and domestic price discrimination laws on the other have tended to diverge in recent years. Price discrimination laws increasingly have recognized the beneficial effects of lower prices on competition and there have been relatively few price discrimination cases. Antidumping laws have been increasingly zealous in attacking unfair foreign trade practices.

National treatment of firms penalized for dumping or price discounting would limit the potential for discrimination between domestic and foreign firms in future. Furthermore, national treatment in price discrimination laws would not require necessarily that each country use the same criteria in applying such laws. As trade barriers are reduced and globalization of the economy proceeds, the application of antidumping laws becomes increasingly bizarre in its effects. Economic logic suggests that antidumping

---

5   This approach has been examined extensively by Lawson Hunter and Douglas Rosenthal in a study prepared for the Committee on Canada-United States Relations of the Canadian Chamber of Commerce and the United States Chamber of Commerce, Feltham, Ivan R., Stuart A. Salen, Robert F. Mathieson, and Ronald Wonnacott, "Competition (Antitrust) and Antidumping Laws in the Context of the Canada-U.S. Free Trade Agreement," 1991.

6   See Bork, R.H., *The Antitrust Paradox: A Policy at War with Itself,* New York, NY: Basic Books, 1978 and Salop, S.C., ed., *Strategy, Predation and Antitrust Analysis,* Washington, DC: Federal Trade Commission, 1981.

will disappear among the three North American economies. Simple logic may not prevail however, and we now turn to a consideration of other approaches.

National treatment raises particularly difficult problems on subsidy issues because neither country has domestic mechanisms to discipline the use and effects of subsidies by various levels of government. In principle, one can argue that subsidies are constrained by government budgets and that governments should be free to engage in domestic subsidies. Yet U.S. import-competing interests, as well as Congress, are unlikely to accept this position, because the prospect of U.S. firms competing with foreign treasuries appears to them to be inherently unfair and raises the spectre of government-supported predatory behaviour.

A basis for applying national treatment to trilateral trade would be an effective trilateral mechanism to discipline and disallow subsidy programs. Such a mechanism could be a better way to deal with bidding rivalries among governments seeking to attract new investment projects. Although controls on these bidding wars would be desirable, U.S. and Canadian legislators likely would be reluctant to cede sovereignty to a supranational agency or tribunal that would have the power to disallow domestic spending programs. Yet, in the absence of such a mechanism, it is going to be very difficult to obtain legislative approval for the national treatment option regarding countervailing duties.

Revised Criteria

The second negotiating approach involves retaining bilateral antidumping mechanisms while revising the criteria by which they are applied. In particular eliminating "sale below cost" provisions in bilateral antidumping laws would remove the most protectionist elements of such laws. Under these existing special provisions, duties may be levied even though no dumping actually occurs. Where companies are not covering their overhead costs in their home market, dumping margins are calculated on the difference between the export price and a "constructed value" based on an estimate of a price that would cover all costs and still yield a normal profit.

Eliminating "sale below cost" provisions in bilateral antidumping laws would bring those laws closer to the standard prevailing in domestic price discrimination laws and would reduce the application of antidumping duties as well as the number of complaints and investigations. At the same time, the incidence of dumping could be reduced by a "boomerang" provision, whereby companies selling a product in the other country cannot prevent, and the originating country must facilitate, the re-export of the product to the producing firms' domestic market.[7] The boomerang provision is one aspect of the European Free Trade Association's (EFTA) rules of competition that could be relevant to the Canadian-U.S. negotiations.

The revised criteria approach is administratively more complicated and lacks the protection against potential abuses of antidumping measures that the national treatment approach provides. However, some may consider it to be an attractive negotiating route because it would avoid the perception that the antidumping system was being dismantled. If antidumping duties were likely to be applied only rarely once tariffs were eliminated, then retaining such mechanisms for bilateral trade could be a relatively costless way to reassure domestic firms that fear being overwhelmed by the reduction of bilateral trade barriers. The risk would still remain, however, that administrative and judicial interpretation of antidumping laws could be subject to a protectionist bias in either or both countries.

A revised definition of a countervailable subsidy could provide greater certainty to producers in one country exporting to the other. One approach is to take seriously the metaphor of the "level playing field," in the sense of focusing on practices that significantly affect the pattern of trade.[8] The objective would be to distinguish between those subsidies that distort trade and those that do not.

Joint Administration

The third possible negotiating approach would involve some form of joint administration of bilateral import relief laws. Joint administration could involve a relatively loose arrangement requiring formal consultation between the two countries before bilateral antidumping duties are imposed. Alternatively, it could involve some variation on the proposal made by the Royal Commission on the Economic Union and Development Prospects for Canada (the Macdonald Commission) to have import relief laws administered by a binational tribunal.

Before examining these alternative approaches, it is important to distinguish between the processes available to industries in either country to seek redress from import competition and the mechanisms for settling disputes between governments that could be developed as a part of a

7   Lambrinidis, J.S., *The Structure, Function and Law of a Free Trade Area: The European Free Trade Association*, New York, NY: Praegar, 1965, p. 149.

8   Lipsey, Richard G., and Murray G. Smith, *Taking the Initiative: Canada's Trade Options in a Difficult World*, Toronto: C.D. Howe Institute, 1985, p. 144.

bilateral agreement. A bilateral agreement almost certainly will create an intergovernmental dispute settlement mechanism, but his mechanism may not replace existing national import relief systems. Nonetheless, developing this type of intergovernmental machinery could help defuse and resolve disputes that now tend to be dealt with under import relief laws.

The goal of developing new bilateral rules regarding subsidies and antidumping and countervailing duty laws was not achieved in the free trade negotiations between Canada and the United States. Canada sought greater security of access to the U.S. market and greater protection from unilateral decisions by U.S. administering agencies that can constrain Canadian exports and constrain the choices of Canadian policymakers. Yet at the same time, the U.S. Congress was seeking to amend U.S. trade legislation to offer domestic industries greater relief from import competition and to provide more effective redress against foreign trade practices perceived to be "unfair."[9] The goal remains since the Free Trade Agreement mandates future negotiations on subsidies and antidumping and countervailing duties.

Provisions of the Free Trade Agreement

The provisions of the Free Trade Agreement (FTA) on these contentious trade policy issues can be described as a stand-off. There was no agreement on new rules to govern antidumping and countervailing duties, but procedural changes were agreed to with respect to the administration of each country's national trade laws. Chapter 19 sets up a new bi-national appeal mechanism, which can replace existing judicial review by the domestic courts of final decisions by the national administering agencies, as well as a review mechanism to monitor changes in antidumping and countervailing duty laws as they apply to the partner country. The objective of these dispute settlement procedures is to provide a more timely appeal mechanism than is available through the courts and to provide joint scrutiny of the decisions taken by the administrative authorities in both countries.[10]

9   See Lipsey, Richard G., and Murray G. Smith, *Global Imbalances and U.S. Policy Responses: A Canadian Perspective*, Washington and Toronto: Canadian-American Committee, 1987; and "Roundtable on U.S. Trade Legislation," in *International Economic Issues*, Halifax: Institute for Research on Public Policy, August 1987.

10   See Steger, Debra, "The Dispute Settlement Mechanisms of the Canada U.S. Free Trade Agreement: Comparison with the Existing System"; Coffield, Shirley, "Dispute Settlement Provisions"; Dearden, Richard, "Antidumping and Countervailing Duty Provisions: Judicial Review by Binational Panels"; and Horlick, Gary, and Debra Valentine, "Improvements in Trade Remedy Law and Procedures under the

Although the softwood lumber dispute influenced the free trade negotiations and the resulting agreement, the understanding on softwood lumber negotiated between Canada and the United States in late 1986 after the preliminary determination by the Department of Commerce was not affected by the FTA. Thus, the issue of stumpage subsidies remained to be resolved either through the future negotiations on subsidies or through the dispute settlement processes under the Agreement. Now that Canada has terminated the softwood lumber memorandum of understanding and the United States has initiated a countervailing duty case against softwood lumber, the application of the dispute settlement processes to this difficult set of issues will be tested.

The free trade negotiations were, however, able to resolve some contentious subsidy issues in other sectors. In the automotive sector, the issue of Canada's export-based duty remission mechanism was resolved in a way which served both Canadian and U.S. objectives, while avoiding a potential U.S. countervailing action which would have been very disruptive to bilateral trade.[11]

In the primary agriculture sector both countries have substantial subsidies (see table 2). Neither country was prepared to dismantle domestic agricultural subsidies on a bilateral basis, because of concerns about the impact on world agricultural markets of the subsidy practices and import restrictions of third countries. However, Canada and the United States did agree to eliminate export subsidies for bilateral trade in agricultural products and Canada has agreed to eliminate import licensing requirements for wheat, oats and barley when subsidy levels in the two countries are equivalent.

The influence of U.S. protectionist pressures was evident in the softwood lumber dispute between Canada and the United States. Although various congressional bills directed against softwood lumber imports did not become law, a change in the interpretation of U.S. countervailing duty law by the U.S. Commerce Department in the 1986 *Softwood Lumber case*, resulted in a negotiated settlement where Canada imposed a 15 percent

Canada-U.S. Free Trade Agreement," in D. McRae, and D. Steger, eds., *Understanding the Free Trade Agreement*, Halifax: Institute for Research on Public Policy, 1988.

11   For an analysis of the implications of the automotive provisions of the FTA, see Wonnacottt, Paul, "The Auto Sector," in Jeffrey J. Schott, and Murray G. Smith, eds., *The Canada United States Free Trade Agreement: The Global Impact*, Washington, DC and Halifax: Institute for International Economics and the Institute for Research on Public Policy, 1988, pp. 101-109.

Table 2
Agricultural Producer Subsidy Equivalents by
Country and Commodity, 1979-88
(selected years) (net percentage PSE)

	1979	1984	1986	1987 (E)	1988 (P)
Canada					
Crops	14	25	54	45	38
Livestock products	31	40	45	47	47
All products	24	33	49	46	43
European Community[a]					
Crops	41	24	67	66	40
Livestock products	45	36	46	45	48
All products	44	33	52	51	46
Japan					
Crops	78	81	93	94	90
Livestock products	45	48	53	55	56
All products	64	67	76	77	74
United States					
Crops	8	21	45	42	34
Livestock products	20	34	41	40	33
All products	15	28	43	41	36

(E) = estimate; (P) = provisional
a. In 1979 and 1984, all present members of the EC except Portugal and Spain.

Source: Organization for Economic Cooperation and Development, *Monitoring and Outlook of Agricultural Policies, Markets and Trade*, Paris, 1989.

export tax on lumber shipped to the United States.[12] The bitter conflict over softwood lumber shaped official attitudes on both sides during the free

---

12   Percy, Michael, and Christian Yoder, *The Softwood Lumber Dispute and Canada-U.S. Trade in Natural Resources*, Halifax: Institute for Research on Public Policy, 1987.

trade negotiations and influenced the agreement that emerged. In effect the Canada-USA FTA seeks to prevent the recurrence of a softwood lumber situation where the administrative interpretation of the trade laws was perceived by Canadians as being altered in response to protectionist pressures. Just as the 1986 softwood lumber dispute shaped Canadian attitudes to the Canada-USA Free Trade negotiations, the outcome of the 1991-92 softwood lumber countervailing duty case will influence Canadian, and also U.S. attitudes, to negotiation of dispute settlement processes for the trade laws in the NAFTA negotiations.

It appears more difficult to generalize the review mechanisms governing the trade laws under Chapter 19. Although there are technical differences, Canadian and U.S. trade laws are remarkably similar. It would be more difficult to apply the Canada-USA Agreement's review mechanism for decisions involving antidumping and countervailing duties to a third country like Mexico whose domestic trade laws and administrative procedures differ substantially from those of the United States and Canada. In particular, it may be difficult to involve Mexico in this type of judicial review, because the Mexican legal system does not have the same basic concepts of administrative law and judicial review, which are common to the Canadian and U.S. legal systems.

Negotiating Internal Measures

The negotiation of import quotas and the trade laws is often linked to internal measures including subsidies, procurement preferences and environmental regulations. Yet the asymmetries in the size and level of development of the three North American economies make it difficult to negotiate any restraints upon domestic policies. Mexicans and also Canadians have often been extremely concerned about the threat to their sovereignty which could arise from U.S. dominance. For its part the United States is likely to resist any restraints on its ability to take unilateral actions.

Subsidies

It proved impossible to agree on disciplines on either agricultural or nonagricultural subsidies in the Canada-USA Free Trade negotiations, and it is likely to be more difficult to develop effective rules limiting the use of domestic subsidies when an economy like Mexico, which has much lower income levels and greater infrastructure needs is added to the negotiations.

It may possible to link liberalization of border measures to progress in limiting subsidies. For example, Mexico may be prepared to liberalize the